BASIC INCOME
The Material Conditions of Freedom

Daniel Raventós

Translated from the Spanish by Julie Wark

Pluto Press
London • Ann Arbor, MI

First published in an earlier version in Spanish, 1999, as *El derecho a la existencia: La propuesta del Subsidio Universal Garantizado* by Editorial Ariel, Barcelona.

English-language edition first published in 2007 by Pluto Press
345 Archway Road, London N6 5AA
and 839 Greene Street, Ann Arbor, MI 48106

www.plutobooks.com

British Library Cataloguing in Publication Data
A catalogue record for this book is available from the British Library

Hardback
ISBN-13   978 0 7453 2630 6
ISBN-10   0 7453 2630 7

Paperback
ISBN-13   978 0 7453 2629 0
ISBN-10   0 7453 2629 3

Library of Congress Cataloging in Publication Data applied for

10 9 8 7 6 5 4 3 2 1

Designed and produced for Pluto Press by
Curran Publishing Services, Norwich

Printed and bound in the European Union by
Anthony Rowe Ltd, Chippenham and Eastbourne, England

BASIC INCOME

For Roger and Teia

CONTENTS

TABLES AND FIGURES

TABLES

FIGURES

[x]

INTRODUCTION AND ACKNOWLEDGEMENTS

In 1999, a first version of this book, *El derecho a la existencia* (The Right to Existence), was published in Spain by Ariel. At the end of 2005 Pluto Press gave me the opportunity to publish it in English. Although much of the original book is still pertinent today, research in the field of Basic Income has greatly benefited from many contributions over these six years and, what with all the political and social changes that have occurred as well, some parts clearly needed to be updated or completely rewritten. Pluto Press has now provided the perfect incentive for revising my original book, which, in its thoroughly reworked version, will be published in Spanish by El Viejo Topo.

Chapter 1 introduces the concept of Basic Income, identifies a number of common confusions, offers a brief account of its history and indicates the very interesting political role it could play at the beginning of the twenty-first century.

Chapter 2 discusses some of the best-known academic theories of justice and reviews the work of such authors as John Rawls, Robert Nozick, Hillel Steiner and Philippe Van Parijs in outlining a number of philosophical justifications of Basic Income.

Chapter 3 will, I hope, offer ground-breaking material for English readers. My description of republicanism and theoretical justification of Basic Income in republican terms is based on ongoing original research (insofar as we can say anything is 'original', of course) I have been engaged in, along with several Catalan and Spanish-speaking colleagues who uphold the idea of republican freedom that is presented here. Republicanism in this book is rather different from the standard fare one finds in academic circles although, of course, our position is closer to the views of some than of others. Within this framework I shall establish a number of connections between the republican defence of Basic Income and some socialist and feminist concerns.

Chapter 4 distinguishes between three kinds of work (remunerated, domestic and voluntary), while pointing out some of the absurdities that can arise when they are confused and when remunerated work is identified as the only kind worthy of the name. A detailed analysis of the relationship between Basic Income and each of the three types of work is also offered.

Chapter 5 looks at different aspects of poverty: how it is measured, the relatively new phenomenon of the working poor, and how poverty affects men and women in different ways. Special attention is given here to the republican idea that the person who is poor is not (cannot be) free.

Chapter 6 presents a view of the welfare state that is rather different from what is found in the conventional literature. There is no getting away from the fact that some of the issues that I raise here will be contentious for those people who favour traditional welfare-state approaches. I also consider how Basic Income compares and contrasts with these ideas.

Chapter 7 constitutes an exhaustive overview of the differences (and similarities, where they exist) between Basic Income and other measures that have either been applied at different times and in different places during the last decade, or that are still on the drawing board as proposals whose supporters are trying to win over citizens and policy makers alike. I believe that this chapter is particularly necessary at a time when a good number of these proposals have been confused with Basic Income because of their supposed similarities.

Chapter 8 deals with the matter of financing Basic Income. This is perhaps one of the areas of Basic Income research where most advances have occurred in the last nine or ten years. Besides some general reflections on financing, I shall discuss in detail one particular proposal with which I am very familiar because I have been part of the research team involved and, more importantly, because it is a financing system that, with due database changes and adjustments appropriate to the fiscal reality of each situation, can be applied in many countries.

Finally, Chapter 9 considers eleven criticisms of Basic Income, offering a detailed response to each of them. Some of these criticisms have already been touched upon in different parts of the book. Others appear here for the first time. I believe this is a good way to reinforce and highlight some aspects of Basic Income that have perhaps not been given enough attention, while also summarising some of the points that are exclusive to this proposal.

Chapters 1, 3, 4, 6 and 8 have been completely rewritten. Chapters 5, 7 and 9 have been considerably modified. Chapter 2, although it has also been subjected to cuts, extensions and, in particular, updating is probably the one that is least changed.

* * *

It is not an easy task to express my gratitude in individual terms to all the people who have inspired ideas, suggested new or further areas of reflection or helped in many other ways in the writing of this book. Any attempt to be exhaustive involves the risk of committing some injustice in the form of omission, yet it would not be very gracious on my part to offer my thanks in general terms alone because there are a lot of people whose contributions must be individually acknowledged for various reasons.

The project of publishing *El derecho a la existencia* in English all began in Valencia in October 2005, thanks to Jurgen de Wispelaere, for whose help I am very grateful. David Castle of Pluto Press worked with me in the early months of 2006, giving shape to the more technical aspects of the book, while Miguel Riera of the Spanish-language publishing house El Viejo Topo has kindly offered all kinds of support.

Julie Wark has translated the book into English. If her task had ended at that, she would already have played a very important role in bringing this book into being. But her contribution has been much greater than this because her knowledge of many of the concerns I have dealt with and her interest in discussing and clarifying some of the finer points have meant that the final result is unquestionably better than the original. Her enthusiastic involvement in the evolution of this book has greatly encouraged me throughout.

Sandra González, Àlex Boso, Paco Ramos, Camila Vollenweider and Daniel Escribano have willingly helped at different stages of the book, checking sources, facts and offering their comments. They have always been there for me when I needed their help.

Jordi Arcarons, my lifelong friend, has helped me inestimably in writing Chapter 8. The fact is that whatever merits the reader may find in the discussion on financing Basic Income in this chapter are mainly his.

María Julia Bertomeu, David Casassas and Jordi Mundó have made some very helpful comments and suggestions on different chapters as I have completed them. I am most grateful to David not only for his help in locating sources but also for the fruits of his long collaboration with me in our work on the theoretical and practical aspects of Basic Income. Again, I have had the great pleasure and privilege of working with these three friends and colleagues in studying, identifying and writing about the specific issues of republicanism in today's world. Anyone who understands that political theory and, still more, political philosophy are not simple intellectual pastimes that are merely part of the process of pursuing a decorous academic career will know what I mean.

In the last 15 years, I have worked more closely with Antoni Domènech than with anyone else in both academic and political domains. His influence on this book, especially with regard to the discussion of republican ideas, is enormous. I share a great deal with Toni, in particular very similar political views and our joint conviction that we have not been mistaken in the essential task of identifying who has been and who is the enemy. If one's intellectual mentor can also be a close friend, then I need say no more about the importance of this relationship.

My brothers, Xavier, Jaume and Sergi, long-time and convinced supporters of Basic Income, have always influenced my work by helping me to hone one argument or another. Many of their concerns, reflections, doubts and suggestions appear in this book.

The influence of Montserrat Cervera on this book is huge because she has constantly and intelligently shared my life for so many years. Her long, genuine and resolute devotion to the causes of feminism and peace, and all the manifestations of her untiring commitment (a peerless example of autotelic activity), to which I have been a privileged witness every day, constitute an inspiring moral and political example and, for this, I am forever in her debt.

Roger, my son, and Teia, Montserrat's daughter, to whom I dedicate this book, belong to a generation which, for many years, will lamentably be forced to confront the terrible inequalities of this world and what they mean in terms of the lack of freedom of millions and millions of people. The world they have inherited could become even worse in future but their generation also has the chance to try to prevent this from happening. Many people before them – and from countless previous generations including my own – have tried to contribute towards creating a better world and many are still trying. Sometimes they are successful. One hopes for further success, not out of some kind of imbecilic optimism but from the standpoint of hope based on reason. I have written *Basic Income: The Material Conditions of Freedom* with this reasoned hope as its driving force.

Barcelona
January 2007

1 A PROVOCATIVE BUT POSSIBLE PROPOSAL

> What is the first object of society? It is to maintain the
> inviolable rights of man. What is the first of these rights?
> The right to exist. The first social law is thus that which
> guarantees to all society's members the means of
> existence; all others are subordinated to it.
>
> Maximilien Robespierre (1758–1794), 1792

The Basic Income proposal has been gathering strength in recent
years, to an extent that may seem surprising. Moreover, it does not
often happen that a social proposal of any magnitude – and this is
one such – should bring together such an array of supporters of
different political leanings, philosophies and countries. It is not
uncommon to find champions of Basic Income among people
who would never have even flirted with the idea of thoroughgoing
change in the societies in which they live, as well as among feminist activists or members of social movements that are clearly
opposed to the status quo. In university circles, too, we find liberals (in the academic rather than the political sense), republicans –
although speaking of 'republicans' and 'liberals' in general terms
is not very helpful – ecologists and feminists once again, along
with many others who are interested in, or in favour of, the Basic
Income proposal. Finally, there are supporters in very different

countries ranging from the United States to Chile, the Kingdom of Spain[1] to Sweden, from Turkey to Australia and South Africa. I shall not start by speculating about whether this diversity represents a virtue of Basic Income, whether it contributes to the confusion about it, or whether it is simply inevitable. We can leave the matter for the moment. I shall have enough space in this book to state what my position is and, I hope, to defend it clearly and precisely.

1.1 THE DEFINITION

What exactly is Basic Income? Before going into detail about the many aspects of the proposal, I should like to offer an unambiguous account of what it is:

> Basic Income is an income paid by the state to each full member or accredited resident of a society, regardless of whether he or she wishes to engage in paid employment, or is rich or poor or, in other words, independently of any other sources of income that person might have, and irrespective of cohabitation arrangements in the domestic sphere.

Although it is somewhat long, this is the definition I prefer because it is clear (and also provocative). The Basic Income Earth Network definition is as follows:

> A basic income is an income unconditionally granted to all on an individual basis, without means test or work requirement. It is a form of minimum income guarantee that differs from those that now exist in various European countries in three important ways:

- it is being paid to individuals rather than households
- it is paid irrespective of any income from other sources
- it is paid without requiring the performance of any work or the willingness to accept a job if offered.[2]

This is also rather a long definition but I shall proceed with the earlier one, which I confess I favour, because it enables me to clarify some points in greater detail.

'*An income paid by the state*'. The word 'state' can cover a juridical-political entity that is larger than existing nation-states, such as the European Union, or it might refer to juridical-political spheres that are smaller than the nation-state, for example autonomously governed territories. Hence, Basic Income is paid by one or more institutions in the public sphere.

'*To each full member or resident of a society*'. In the different models for financing Basic Income there are variations in the amount paid, according to age, or whether minors are included in the policy or not, and so on. However, in all cases, this is a sum of money that citizens receive as individuals (and not by family groups, for example), and universally (not dependent on, say, predetermined thresholds of poverty).

'*Regardless of whether he or she wishes to engage in paid employment*'. For the present, it is sufficient to note that 'work' is all too often understood as 'paid employment' or 'job'. There are good reasons for thinking that the following typology is more appropriate: (1) paid work in the labour market, (2) domestic work, and (3) voluntary work. These distinctions are important, as I shall explain in Chapter 4.

'*Whether he or she ... is rich or poor or, in other words, independently of any other sources of income that person might have*'. Unlike means-tested subsidies that depend on defined levels of poverty or types of situation, Basic Income is received by rich and poor alike.[3] If it is conceived as a right of citizenship (as the definition suggests), that excludes any additional condition. Like the right of universal suffrage, the Basic Income proposal does not impose any conditions beyond citizenship (or accredited residence).

'*Irrespective of cohabitation arrangements in the domestic sphere*'. Basic Income does not favour or penalise any particular form of cohabitation. It makes no difference whether a heterosexual couple, people from different generations, a group of friends or a homosexual couple live under the same roof. These are all ways of living together that are completely independent of the right to receive a Basic Income.

Basic Income, then, is formally secular, unconditional and universal. It would be received by each and every member of the society irrespective of gender, level of income, religion and sexual orientation. In this distinctive feature of not being conditional upon any requisite other than citizenship or accredited residence, Basic Income is incontrovertibly very different from other proposals, whether they have been applied in practice for years or whether they have never gone beyond the state of 'theory'. Let us look more closely now at this distinctiveness.

1.2 WHAT BASIC INCOME IS NOT

In making clear what Basic Income is not, it is important to note at this introductory stage some other, supposedly similar measures with which Basic Income should not be confused. This does not mean making any kind of comparative evaluation at this point because I shall do this in Chapter 6. For the moment, I think it is only necessary to offer a very brief account of measures, whether still on the drawing board or already put into practice, which need to be distinguished from

Basic Income even though some of them would appear at first sight to be quite similar.

Basic Income is not participation income, a proposal that was made by Anthony Atkinson (1993, 1996) and others. This is the payment of a sum of money to all citizens who are able to work and who are engaged in some kind of activity that is deemed socially useful. This 'socially useful activity' might include remunerated employment, voluntary work, domestic labour, studying and so on.

Neither should Basic Income be confused with negative income tax (NIT). This is a uniform, refundable tax that guarantees a minimum income through taxation policy. If this minimum income level is exceeded in the tax declaration, the corresponding taxes must be paid. If the minimum level is not exceeded or there is no income, the state pays the difference in order to make up the minimum stipulated level.

Basic Income is not what is known in Spain as *Rentas Mínimas de Inserción* (RMI – minimum income support), which is paid (to less than 1 per cent of the population) by most of the country's 17 (or 19 if we include the enclaves of Ceuta and Melilla in North Africa) autonomous communities. In France, under the name of *Revenu Minimum d'Insertion*, it is paid by the central government. The aim, according to RMI enthusiasts, is to achieve a coordinated development of activities so as to help people who do not have the economic resources to meet their basic needs, and to prepare them to enter the job market and social life. These activities include making social services available, and providing economic assistance and personal support in their integration into the workplace and society.

Basic Income should not be confused, either, with any kind of temporary unemployment benefit or dole system whereby an individual receives payment from the state as long as she or he is unable to find paid work but, once a job is found, the payment stops.

In brief, Basic Income is not a grant, subsidy or conditioned unemployment benefit of any kind, because the only requisite for receiving it is citizenship or accredited residence.

1.3   IS THERE A BASIC INCOME ANYWHERE IN THE WORLD?

Since 1982, or for the last quarter of a century, anyone legally residing in the State of Alaska for more than six months has been receiving a Basic Income. At present some 700,000 people meet this condition of legal residency. The name most closely associated with this story is that of Jay Hammond, who died in 2005. He was Governor of Alaska for eight years, from 1974 to 1982. The state is rich in oil, the Prudhoe Bay field being the biggest in the United States, and Hammond proposed that this wealth should benefit the population, present and future, by means of a fund, consisting of part of the oil revenue, which would guarantee the continuity of the benefits. The Alaska Permanent Fund was created to this end in 1976.

In the early days of the project, Hammond proposed that a dividend should be paid each year to everyone who met the conditions of residence, with the proviso that the dividend paid should be proportional to the number of years of residence. The Supreme Court of the United States then pronounced that the proposal was incompatible with the Equal Protection Clause of the Fourteenth Amendment of the United States Constitution. The Fourteenth Amendment guarantees equal protection of the law to anyone who may be within the territorial jurisdiction of a state. Its terms imply that equal treatment cannot be denied to anyone on the grounds of how long that person has been within the jurisdiction of the state, and the Supreme Court ruled that residents coming from other states were being discriminated against. Modifications were made to get around this objection, after which a Basic Income was introduced for the first time in 1982. It was a true Basic Income, for all the singularity of the territory where it was introduced.[4]

The Alaska Basic Income is a dividend that corresponds to part of the average performance over the previous five years of the permanent fund that is based on oil revenue. The fund has undergone numerous modifications and presently consists of a portfolio that has been diversified on a worldwide scale. Alaska's Basic Income represented a total of $2000 for every resident in 2000. If recent decades have seen a steady redistribution of wealth in the United States in favour of the richest members of society (Frank, 1999; Stiglitz, 2003), Alaska continues to move in the opposite direction so that it is 'the most egalitarian' of all the states in the USA (Vanderborght and Van Parijs, 2005). Basic Income in Alaska is not provided in the form that I find most satisfactory in theoretical and political terms, especially because of the way it is financed. I believe that a Basic Income should be financed differently, as I shall discuss at length in Chapter 8. However, the Alaskan scheme is the only Basic Income that is functioning in any real terms in the world today.

1.4   HISTORICAL PRECEDENTS

The term 'Basic Income' is not unanimously accepted by everyone who has supported, criticised or debated this social initiative. In books and articles, the same proposal is referred to in different ways, among them social dividend, guaranteed universal subsidy and citizenship income. The fact that quite a range of different proposals have also been presented under the name of Basic Income has only increased the confusion.

The historical roots of Basic Income go back quite a long

way.[5] Authors of very different intellectual persuasions have contributed proposals, ideas and debates that, while none of them can remotely be described as a proto-Basic Income, do offer precedents that should at least be borne in mind from a historical perspective. A general connection may even be found in *Utopia* (1516) by Thomas More (1478–1535). This was a long time ago, however, and the relations are tenuous, as are those we might find in the writings of his contemporary, the Catalan thinker Joan Lluís Vives (1492–1540). More recent, and more interesting in my view, though still quite a long time ago, is the case of Thomas Paine (1737–1809). This English revolutionary, son of working-class Quakers, who arrived in Philadelphia at the end of 1774, was an activist in both the American and French revolutions. In 1796 he wrote in his pamphlet *Agrarian Justice*:

> In advocating the case of the persons thus dispossessed, it is a right, and not a charity, that I am pleading for. ... To create a national fund, out of which there shall be paid to every person, when arrived at the age of twenty-one years, the sum of fifteen pounds sterling, as a compensation in part, for the loss of his or her natural inheritance, by the introduction of the system of landed property: [a]nd also, the sum of ten pounds per annum, during life, to every person now living, of the age of fifty years, and to all others as they shall arrive at that age. ... It is proposed that the payments, as already stated, be made to every person, rich or poor.[6]

This sounds familiar. Around this time we find authors who have referred to what I shall call, for want of a better expression, a proto-Basic Income. Notable among these are Thomas Spence (1750–1814), Charles Fourier (1772–1837), Herbert

Spencer (1820–1903) and Henry George (1839–97). More recent is Bertrand Russell (1872–1970) who wrote:

> Stated in more familiar terms, the plan we are advocating amounts essentially to this: that a certain small income, sufficient for necessaries, should be secured to all, whether they work or not, and that a larger income, as much larger as might be warranted by the total amount of commodities produced, should be given to those who are willing to engage in some work which the community recognises as useful.[7]

Some well-known economists, too, have written about what we might also call a proto-Basic Income, among them James Meade (1907–1995) and James Tobin (1918–2002), winners of the Nobel Prize for Economics in 1977 and 1981 respectively.

More recently, in the 1960s, there were a number of developments in the United States that are closely related to Basic Income. One of the most famous neoliberal economists of the 1970s and 1980s, though now in marked decline in terms of any intellectual influence (I refer, of course, to the recently deceased Milton Friedman (1912–2006)), proposed a 'negative income tax' (see Section 1.2 above) in his famous book *Capitalism and Freedom* (1962). In 1965, James Tobin proposed a guaranteed minimum income, this representing an unquestionable improvement over the then-existing welfare programmes in the United States. There is a huge difference in motivation between Friedman and Tobin. If the former aimed to dismantle the welfare state, the latter aspired to improve the conditions of the economically disadvantaged members of society and to bring an end to poverty in his country. Again, the Republican administration of President Richard Nixon drew up reforms that included a guaranteed income in combination with a family assistance plan for workers, the proposals for this taking the form of negative income tax. The plan was debated in the Senate until Nixon resigned from office under threat of impeachment in November 1974 following the resounding Watergate scandal. The initial impetus of negative income tax soon fizzled out. Meanwhile, in Canada too, negative income tax was being considered and interest in the proposal lasted until well into the 1980s.[8]

1.5 THE LAST 20 YEARS

In the 1970s and early 1980s, there were several significant advances in Basic Income thinking, though they were largely independent of each other,[9] but 1986 is a particularly significant year. The 'Charles Fourier Collective', a group of researchers and trade unionists associated with the University of Louvaine, had presented a paper entitled '*L'allocation universelle*' (Basic Income) two years previously. A congress, funded by a major Belgian prize that was awarded to this work, was organised at the university in 1986, bringing together a number of researchers from different countries, all of whom had begun to work on the idea of Basic Income. It was at this congress that a decision was made to create the Basic Income European Network (BIEN) and, 20 years later, there can be no doubt as to its importance in the history of Basic Income. BIEN has held ten congresses since then: 1988 (Antwerp, Belgium); 1990 (Florence, Italy); 1992 (Paris, France); 1994 (London, United Kingdom); 1996 (Vienna, Austria); 1998 (Amsterdam, Holland); 2000 (Berlin, Germany); 2002 (Geneva, Switzerland); 2004 (Barcelona, Spain) and 2006 (Cape Town, South Africa).

The 2004 Barcelona congress brought another major change. Until the Ninth Congress in Geneva, BIEN had been, as its name suggests, restricted to Europe. At the Tenth Congress in

Barcelona it was decided to transform BIEN into the Basic Income Earth Network. Students and activists from non-European countries had been asking to be included in the Network and the only way to do this was by turning the European network into a worldwide network. And, after all, in the previous few years, an increasing number of people from outside the Old Continent had started attending the BIEN congresses. Before 2004, Basic Income groups had appeared in the United States, South America, South Africa, Australia and New Zealand. The first congress of the Basic Income Earth Network as a worldwide association was hosted in November 2006 by Cape Town, South Africa. At present (early 2007), there are 12 officially recognised BIEN sections from four continents: Germany, Argentina, Austria, Brazil, United States, United Kingdom, Spain, Switzerland, Ireland, Holland, Australia and Denmark.

In the more than 20 years since BIEN was founded, the world has changed in very significant ways. To limit myself to just a few important facts, the president of the United States in 1986 was Ronald Reagan, while Margaret Thatcher was prime minister of Great Britain, both of them champions of what is more or less aptly named neoliberalism; dictators who were also supporters of neoliberal programmes were in power in Latin America and subjugating their populations with regimes of terror (Chile, under the Pinochet boot, was perhaps the clearest case); the still-surviving USSR was teetering at the peak of its crisis while, in many other parts of the world, neoliberalism was rampant (by neoliberalism I mean the openly expressed objective of favouring the rich with the argument that this is indisputably good not only for this minority but also for the whole of society, a case which, it must be said, convinced a not-inconsiderable part of the left). One can't help thinking of the observation of Frank Zappa (1940–1993) that politics is industry's department of show business.

These were also times of crisis for the less complacent members of the left. There was no trace of a socialist paradise in what the populations of the USSR and so-called Eastern Europe suffered under the yoke of bureaucratic castes that dominated the political sphere, nor did the wonders promised by neoliberal zealots bear any relation to the increasingly harsh conditions that the working class and less-privileged population in general had to endure. In what was then called Western Europe, unemployment figures rocketed to levels not seen for many years and it was precisely in the 1980s that they reached unthinkable extremes in this placid post-war part of the world.

This was the context in which BIEN appeared. The Basic Income proposal was a beacon in this sombre setting where ideas were mainly notable for their insipid lack of originality.

1.6 BASIC INCOME IN THE TWENTY-FIRST CENTURY

Twenty years on, the USSR no longer exists and neither do its former Eastern European satellite regimes; neoliberalism no longer inspires the same fervent support because its disturbingly negative results cannot be disguised, and Latin America now has several democratic governments, some more and some less left-wing but all determined to resist the neoliberal assault. In a context so different from that of two decades ago, Basic Income could play, and I believe is playing, a very interesting political role. I shall discuss this below after highlighting two further points.

First, 20 years ago, the concept of Basic Income was virtually limited to academic circles and had little impact beyond them. This is no longer the case. The Basic Income proposal is now well known (although not nearly so widely accepted) in trade union, social and political circles. Second, 20 years ago interest in Basic Income was confined, with very few exceptions, to Europe. Today, the Basic Income proposal, though it may be given different names, is no longer a stranger in non-European countries, as we have seen.

This interest in Basic Income in countries like Argentina, Brazil, South Africa, Mexico and Colombia, which cannot in any way be seen as belonging to the select group of the rich countries, is not coincidental, I believe. Let us not forget that between 1980 – not long before BIEN was established – and 2000, the average per capita GDP of the rich (or developed) countries rose from US$20,000 to US$30,000 per annum (at 1995 constant-dollar rates), while in the poor (or underdeveloped) countries it dropped from US$65 to US$257. In other words, over the last two decades of the twentieth century, while GDP per capita rose in the former group by 50 per cent, the countries of the latter group were not even able to maintain their already meagre standard of life. Another way of putting it is that the per capita GDP of rich countries is now over 120 times greater than that of poor countries. Whatever way you look at it, the difference is staggering.

This brings me to the fascinating political role that Basic Income could play now, at the beginning of the twenty-first century. I have already referred to some very interesting aspects of Basic Income, namely its formal features of being secular, unconditional and universal, which coincide exactly with those of democratic universal suffrage where the right to vote is independent of gender, ethnic group of origin, level of income, sexual choice or professed religion. The great struggles for universal suffrage and democracy in the nineteenth century and the first third of the twentieth century by working populations – who were excluded by means of the limited-census suffrage agreed upon by nineteenth-century conservatives and liberals alike – certainly had a good dose of instrumentality, because achieving democracy was seen as a step along the way to other goals (socialism, redistributive justice and so on). Yet the struggle for universal suffrage was much more than an instrumental project, because the universality and unconditional nature of the right to vote ended up bestowing upon these populations value in and for themselves, however much the very anti-democratic nineteenth-century liberals and conservatives brayed in distress that the consequences would be dire.

I believe that the struggle for a citizens' Basic Income could now play a similar role. There is, of course, an instrumental side to this since the aim is to do away with poverty and to put an end to neoliberal policies or, in less abstract terms, to ensure that the greater part of the world's population no longer has to subsist in conditions of the direst poverty and at the mercy of the caprices of the very few who are rich. Yet Basic Income can also be non-instrumental as an inalienable right of justice and dignity and as a value in itself, and the act of demanding it could crystallise in the formation of social movements and democratic public opinion, however much the very anti-democratic twenty-first-century neoconservatives bray in distress that the consequences will be dire.

One of the great moral strengths of supporting Basic Income is that it not only draws attention to evidence of the appalling inequalities of the contemporary world but also, and in particular, to the erosion of freedom that goes hand-in-hand with huge disparities of income and wealth. Equality and freedom are not two goals to be chosen independently of one another. Great social inequalities are a real impediment to the freedom of many millions of people, while the other side of the coin is that the lack of freedom of so many people, the increasingly compelling need for working populations to ask permission of the rich every day in order to continue subsisting in conditions dictated by their masters, only aggravates inequality.

Poverty is not only privation, material want and income disparity. It also means dependence on the arbitrary whims and greed of others, lack of self-esteem, isolation and the social compartmentalisation of the poor. Anyone whose material existence is increasingly unsure also suffers the corresponding erosion of his or her freedom (in the form of 'first-job contracts', temporary contracts, absence of contracts, precariousness, job 'flexibility' and outright unemployment without any social protection whatsoever). This erosion of freedom then redounds on the growth of material inequality (in the form of decreases in real salaries, insecure retirement pensions, privatised or pauperised public services and infrastructure, and so on, while financial and corporative profits remain sky-high). This material inequality also affects the most powerful country on Earth, to an extent that even supporters of the status quo now find hard to justify. One only needs to glance at what the veteran University of Maryland professor Gar Alperovitz pointed out in an article published at the beginning of 2006.[10] The richest 2.5 million people in the United States earn more than twice the combined income of more than 100 million people. Another way of putting it is that 1 per cent of the population has twice the combined income of the bottom 34 per cent! This tremendous inequality cannot but affect the freedom of the vast majority.

1.7 STRENGTHS, QUESTIONS, DOUBTS

While Basic Income has been associated with a series of advantages it has also raised doubts and questions. I shall give a brief account of the advantages before dealing at length with doubts and questions elsewhere in the book.

Basic Income totally eliminates the blight of stigmatisation.

Since it is a universal right for everyone and only conditional on citizenship or residence, there can be no stigma because everyone receives it.

Basic Income allows greater flexibility in the job market, but this flexibility also offers considerable protection for the worker. It would provide greater freedom in choosing a job and, very importantly, it makes one crucial choice possible: that of not working for a wage. Some writers, following in the footsteps of Marx (for example Erik Olin Wright, 2006), call this 'decommodification of labour'. Again, it offers greater opportunities to choose the organisational form of wage labour (self-employment and cooperatives, for example) that one wishes to engage in.

Basic Income avoids poverty and unemployment traps. These traps appear because the monetary amounts of conditional subsidies are not cumulative: that is to say they supplement an already existing income only up to a pre-established ceiling, and hence there is no incentive to accept part-time employment or any kind of paid work. Technically, this might be expressed as follows: the marginal tax rate is, in many cases, 100 per cent. This means that for each monetary unit of paid income that might be obtained, one monetary unit of unemployment benefits is lost. In brief, the poverty and unemployment traps appear when payment of monetary or other kinds of benefits is conditional upon the authorities being able to verify the insufficiency of income received within the job market. Unlike conditioned subsidies, Basic Income does not constitute a ceiling but simply defines a basic level of income beyond which people are free to accumulate any other kind of income. Basic Income, since it is unconditional and perfectly compatible with other sources of income (including remunerated work), would circumvent the poverty trap. (The unemployment trap is a special case within the poverty trap, occurring in situations where it makes better financial sense not to accept a job than to take it and, as a result, lose the unemployment benefits.)

Basic Income permits other kinds of distribution of labour as we shall see in more detail in Chapter 4. People would be freer to decide how and when they would provide their labour in exchange for a salary, whether they would prefer to do voluntary work or to devote their time to reproductive or domestic labour. Again, Basic Income takes the edge off aversion to risk and enables greater innovation. There are generally two kinds of people who want to set up small businesses: those that are cushioned (mostly by the family), in which case they can set up a business project rationally and steadily, and those for whom some kind of self-employment is the only job possibility. In these cases, the risk is not only that of losing the initial investment but also the means of subsistence, which makes any employment decision more anxiety ridden. Not only this, but in many cases lack of initial capital puts off potential small entrepreneurs. Basic Income would help them to capitalise the business project while, at the same time, they would not be so dependent on its success in order to survive.

Basic Income undercuts, though without abolishing, the power of the capitalist in the labour relation. Negotiating power and strategies of work relations change because the weaker party becomes stronger. This is not to suggest that any relationship of equality is established between the two parties in the work situation because the capitalist or his or her representative still defines the content, form and conditions (economic included) of the workers' labour, while maintaining management powers almost intact. One effect of this greater bargaining power for workers would be that capitalists would have to offer pay rises and improved working conditions to make the least appealing and most monotonous jobs more attractive, because nobody would feel obliged to accept them in order to survive. The average pay of more attractive and intrinsically gratifying jobs would also conceivably drop.

Are all these advantages for real? When someone looks into the Basic Income proposal for the first time a lot of questions and doubts usually appear. The answers to these may lead to other, perhaps more sophisticated, questions and doubts. Some are normative (referring to aspects concerned with the intrinsic justice of the proposal), while others are more technical (regarding practical matters, in particular but not exclusively the financial aspects). What kind of intellectual resistance does a proposal like Basic Income encounter? Is the proposal just? Does somebody who doesn't want to work have a right to an unconditional allowance? Would it mean the end of poverty? Isn't the welfare state system of means-tested subsidies better? Can Basic Income be financed? Would people work if they received a Basic Income? Wouldn't it be better to guarantee the right to work? Would workers have better bargaining power with a Basic Income? How would Basic Income affect the phenomenon of poor immigrants from poor countries coming in great numbers to rich countries? Should women be interested in Basic Income? Some people even wonder whether Basic Income would merely be a sugar coating on the bitter pill of capitalism or if it could become part of a socialist project.

I shall deal in detail with all these questions and others in the chapters to come.

2 NORMATIVE LIBERAL JUSTIFICATIONS

> The law, in its majestic equality, forbids the rich as well as the poor to sleep under bridges, to beg in the streets, and to steal bread.
>
> Anatole France (1844–1924), 1894

At the end of Chapter 1, I asked whether the Basic Income proposal is just. Some people prefer a less precise formulation of the question and ask: 'Is Basic Income ethical?' We all have our own, distinctive moral standards. Some might be not very highly elaborated, some very sophisticated and others difficult to defend. Ethics is closely related to morality but the two are not the same. Ethics might be defined as 'the critical analysis of moral laws or content and the elaboration of rational criteria for choosing among moral alternatives' (Mosterín, 2006: 370).[1]

I believe that it is more appropriate to speak of justice rather than ethics when we are referring to Basic Income. And the justice or lack of it in any social proposal is the stuff of theories of justice, so questioning the justice or otherwise of Basic Income is highly relevant. Any politically or economically viable social measure would be of little use if it were not desirable in terms of justice. One example of this might be a proposal that remunerated jobs should be preferentially allocated to males aged between 25 and 45 years. There is nothing very difficult in making such a proposal technically viable, but ethically it would not be what we understand by a just social measure. While it is true that in practice one should not excessively separate normative desirability from political and economic viability (Basic Income has no chance of success if it is not perceived as a just and ethically acceptable measure across a good part of the social spectrum), it is conceptually hygienic to do so. Cheerfully and carelessly mixing the two spheres does not offer much theoretical clarity on the matter.

The strongest objection that might be made against Basic Income is not that it would be impossible to finance but that it is not just. There are different approaches to constructing a normative foundation for Basic Income and I shall do so on the basis of several theories of justice. First, however, I want to note that there are people who are attracted by the proposal because they see it as a lesser evil. We might for instance mention those who think that Basic Income might be a way of preventing the plight of the poor from becoming so explosive that it endangers the social order. Others see Basic Income as an opportunity or measure that would make them more 'justified' in demanding privatisation of the public health and education sectors, and there are other examples. However, I do not wish to evaluate the theoretical and political consistency of this kind of 'defence' of Basic Income, but simply to offer a couple of clear examples of what I mean by such pragmatic support. The theories of justice that attempt to justify Basic Income endeavour to go somewhat further, or much further, than these 'defences' of Basic Income as a lesser evil. The first step is to specify a certain conception of what is (or is not) socially just.

Any normative theory of justice is committed to some particular form of equality as distinct from other forms. In 1992, Amartya Sen, the 1998 Nobel Prize Laureate in Economics, was at pains to show that any defence of equality is carried out in terms of some or other variable and, evidently, variables differ from one author to another. Therefore, when we talk about equality we should also talk about the kind of equality we are upholding. More precisely, equality of what? Proclaiming the desire for greater equality per se is not, to say the least, very enlightening. Without clear elucidation of exactly what kind of equality is considered good, just or desirable, we are moving in the mists of vagueness.

Different writers who share this view differ with regard to choosing the criterion for equality, or dispute which variable should be designated. Among the best-known writers in the field of political philosophy over the past 40 years we find some who determine access to primary goods as the foremost variable of equality (John Rawls), some who opt for equality in possession of internal and external resources (Ronald Dworkin), and still others who prefer equality in basic capacities, as in the case of Amartya Sen. Even normative theories that are quite rightly seen as scarcely egalitarian, a relevant case being that of Robert Nozick (1938–2002), still have to be seen as having some egalitarian features. For Nozick, in his defence of libertarianism, the relevant egalitarian criterion is that pertaining to individual property rights. For him, any form of equality that violates or jeopardises these rights is not just. If, for example, in wanting to redistribute resources, we do not respect individual property rights, Nozick would say we are committing an injustice. Hence, a theory can accept that many inequalities exist in other spheres or variables as long as there is respect for the form of equality that is deemed essential. Any diversion from this criterion – and as I have said the criterion depends on the theory we are looking at – would mean that the society in question is not just.

Finally, 'equality in everything' is an absurd notion. Sen points out, 'The demand for equality in terms of one variable entails that the theory concerned may have to be non-egalitarian with respect to another variable, since the two perspectives can, quite possibly, conflict.'[2] I shall now take a closer look at some of the more substantial theories of justice and at how they might justify the social proposal of Basic Income, starting with a liberal theory of individual property, in Robert Nozick's libertarian view.[3]

2.1 THE LIBERTARIAN JUSTIFICATION: PROPERTY FIRST

Libertarian political philosophy in the closing quarter of the twentieth century, mainly based on the work of Robert Nozick (1974), has been a great success in both academic and real-world terms. Nozick influenced and continues to influence advocates of a maximum dismantling of state forms of social protection, while his theory is also wielded by implacable enemies of property regulation and, still more, of any kind of redistribution of income from the rich to the poor. With regard to my earlier reference to the practical success of Nozick's political philosophy, the briefest glace at what has been happening in the world over the past three decades might indicate the 'realisation' of his postulates. This said, I must allow that his political philosophy is one of indisputable sophistication.

Nozick's brand of libertarianism asserts that individuals have inalienable rights, which might be summed up as property rights. According to this theory, any society that satisfies certain principles in this regard is just. These principles are: (1) respect for property rights; (2) respect, as defined by Locke's proviso, for the 'original appropriation' of external resources;[4] and (3) respect for the results deriving from freely consented exchanges of goods and services. If we find a society that has not respected one or more of these principles, Nozick considers that it is necessary (4) to go ahead with reparations that rectify the violations, over the course of history, of any of the postulates of the theory. In other words, he prescribes going back in time to trace the successive transfers until it is possible to confirm or deny that that original acquisition was legitimate.

At the nucleus of this theory of justice are three basic principles in Nozick's liberal theory of property. The first, pertaining to transfers, states that anything that has been acquired justly can be freely transferred. The second is the principle of initial just acquisition, which is to say an account of how people have come, from the beginning, to have all the things that can be transferred in accordance with the first principle. Finally, the third principle refers to the rectification of injustice and proposes a criterion for action with regard to something that has been possessed through unjust acquisition or transfer.

If we pay close attention to the three principles, we can see that Nozick's theory of justice would oppose rectifying the circumstances that lead to starting-point inequalities. One of the reasons for this rejection is what is known as the 'slippery slope' argument. In this view, it is not denied that social inequalities exist (although supporters of this theory tend to use the term 'disadvantages' rather than 'inequalities'), brought about by different circumstances. Furthermore, so the argument goes, it is not difficult to see that there are numerous natural disadvantages. Some people are much more intelligent than others, some have more delightful social graces, while others have irresistible sexual appeal, and so on. If we begin by trying to rectify some certainly unjustifiable social disadvantages, this would be followed by rectifications of other disadvantages or inequalities that might be more justifiable, and so on to interventions against natural inequalities. The 'slippery slope' could lead to an appalling ending: the advent of central planning or utterly abusive social interventions that would seek to rectify natural inequalities. If these prophets of doom had the literary gifts of a Kurt Vonnegut (1922–2007) they might describe their *reductio ad absurdum* nightmare in terms similar to his memorable story 'Harrison Bergeron' (1968):

> [E]verybody was finally equal. ... Nobody was smarter than anybody else. Nobody was better looking than anybody else. Nobody was stronger or quicker than anybody else. All this equality was due to the 211th, 212th, and 213th Amendments to the Constitution, and to the unceasing vigilance of agents of the United States Handicapper General.

The theoretician who was most eloquent in opposing rectification of social disadvantages – a little over 50 years ago – was Friedrich Von Hayek (1899–1992), while the 'slippery slope' is a variant on the risk thesis propounded by Alfred Hirschman (1995), according to which, even though a proposed change may be desirable, it implies unacceptable costs or consequences. These libertarians want to know where to draw the line that will ensure that we do not end up sliding into totally undesirable situations, using the 'slippery slope' as a grim warning against any kind of rectifying intervention by the state. Will Kymlicka (1990: 155) sagely notes that:

> until we can find a clear and acceptable line between choices and circumstances, there will be some discomfort at making these forms of unfairness the basis of enforceable claims. Libertarianism capitalizes on that discomfort by suggesting that we can avoid having to draw that line.

I am not so much interested here in a discussion of the principles on which Nozick's influential property-based theory rests, but rather how it would justify Basic Income. It may seem startling that a normative theory that is so opposed to rectification of social circumstances can offer some justification of Basic Income, but another well-known libertarian, Hillel Steiner, has produced a theory to do just that.

Steiner (1992) departs from the assumption that the original common ownership of the Earth and, more generally, of its natural resources is equally shared by all human beings. He says that although the fruits of labour should not be taxed, the fruits of Nature should be, because natural resources are not initially the property of any one person or group. A just tax takes from people what they do not have a right to possess. One has an absolute right, according to libertarianism, to make whatever one wishes of oneself and to do what one likes with the goods that are one's legitimate property but, as we have said, natural resources are not, in principle, the property of anyone in particular and, moreover, everyone has an equal right to them. Each person is the owner of goods he or she has legitimately acquired and taxes cannot be imposed on these, to attempt some kind of redistribution, for example. However, goods also contain natural resources over which, in Steiner's view, everybody has a moral right. It is perfectly in keeping with libertarian principles to effect an egalitarian redistribution of the part of the global income that corresponds to the value arising from the incorporation of natural resources into private goods. A tax on natural resources would therefore be just. There are two other taxes that are just for a libertarian: inheritance taxes and taxes on genetic endowments. Steiner compares these with natural resources and, as a result they too would be subject to redistribution.

Independently of the practical difficulties of taxing genetic endowments, for example, we have here a libertarian justification for Basic Income. It is evident that Nature cannot be redistributed (not even in the form of small plots of land) among the almost

7 billion people who inhabit the planet in mid-2007, but it is possible to effect an approximation that could substitute for the natural distribution. This is where the justification of Basic Income comes in. For libertarians, this redistribution would mean introducing a 'single tax' at a level that would cover land rent as determined by a hypothetical perfect market. Since it is impossible to effect a hypothetical redistribution of natural resources to everyone, this must be replaced by some kind of income. In Steiner's view (1992: 89), a Basic Income must be universal if it is to be compatible with libertarian principles.

2.2 THE 'POSSIBLE' JUSTIFICATION OF JUSTICE AS FAIRNESS: SELF-RESPECT TO THE FORE

Before I proceed to the liberal justification (sometimes dubbed egalitarian or solidarity-based) of Basic Income in terms of the theory of justice formulated by John Rawls (1921–2002), it must be stressed that what follows is not what Rawls himself says about Basic Income. Rawls never said he was in favour of Basic Income. On the contrary, in an article of 1988, he unambiguously stated that his theory of justice did not admit of a Basic Income. This was when he used the provocative example of Malibu surfers, saying that they are not entitled to be maintained by public funds. Should we deduce from this that Basic Income is not justifiable in the terms of the theory of justice as fairness? Vanderborght and Van Parijs (2005: 74) are quite specific when they state that, 'it is impossible to deny categorically that a Basic Income can be justified on the basis of Rawls's theory, just as it is impossible to affirm categorically that it can be.' Nonetheless, I shall, although tentatively, take the position that it is possible to justify Basic Income on the basis of Rawls's theory (1971).

What Rawls called the 'circumstances of justice' are those normal conditions under which human cooperation is both possible and necessary. He divides them into objective and subjective circumstances (1971, 2001). Among the former, Rawls cites moderate scarcity and the need for social cooperation, while the latter are those pertaining to people who work together. In brief, the circumstances of justice include moderate scarcity and conflict of interests since without these justice would not be necessary. If natural and non-natural resources existed in exuberant profusion, any plans for cooperation would surely be superfluous. When any particular good exists in great abundance, conflict deriving from the struggle for possessing it tends to diminish or disappear.[5] Rawls was concerned to make this very clear.

What is to be distributed according to the theory of justice as fairness, and what criteria should govern such a distribution? To answer the first part of the question, what must be distributed is the set of primary goods that enable people to promote their different conceptions of what constitutes a good life.[6] These primary goods that play such an important role in the theory of justice as fairness are rights, freedoms and opportunities, along with income and wealth. Self-respect must also be included. Self-respect, as we shall see, is a primary good that would have a prominent place in any justification of Basic Income based on the theory of justice as fairness. So important is self-respect in this normative theory that it would be a good idea to give a brief account here of what Rawls understood by it. Self-respect includes, first of all, the sense of one's own value, the feeling that one's life project deserves to be carried out and, second, confidence in one's own power to bring one's personal intentions into effect. Without self-respect, nothing seems worthy of attempting, and even if any projects should have some value for a person who lacks self-respect, he or she will not have the necessary willpower to carry them out.

Primary goods, as defined in the theory, represent an extremely heterogeneous set, so that it is difficult to make any kind of index of them. The only way of aggregating such heterogeneous magnitudes and creating an index of primary goods is to assign an order of lexicographic priorities.[7] Although we cannot compare the primary goods with each other because of their heterogeneity, we can establish a hierarchy: first, liberties, next, equality of opportunities, and then income. What is to be distributed is thereby based on a lexicographic index of primary goods.

Once we know what is to be distributed, the criterion for distribution is still to be determined. This is given the name of 'leximin'. The principles of the theory of justice as fairness, which have almost become a commonplace after so much repetition, are that any person must have an equal right to the widest possible set of equal freedoms that would be compatible with a set of freedoms for everyone. Tolerable social and economic inequalities have to satisfy two conditions. First, they must somehow work in favour of the most disadvantaged members of society and, second, they must be incorporated into functions and positions that are open to all in conditions of fair equality of opportunities. In other words, Rawls's proposal can be schematically stated as follows, in keeping with the leximin criterion:

1. The first criterion by which a society should be organised is that of a maximum of public freedoms for all.
2. The second criterion of social organisation is that of fair equality in opportunities of access to public positions, meaning that nobody can be discriminated against on grounds of gender, race, class, culture and the like.
3. Finally, according to the third criterion, the organisation of a society must be based on a distribution of wealth that would maximise the income of the most disadvantaged

members. It must *maxi*mise for those that have the *mimi*mum income. This is the *maximin* criterion.[8] This criterion indicates that inequalities of wealth that benefit the least privileged members of society are tolerable. The benefit might arise from the fact that economic inequalities contribute towards the efficiency of the economy.

The restrictions imposed by the leximin criterion are considerable. Thus, for example, no sacrifice of public freedoms in favour of greater distributive equality would be permitted. Neither can greater equality of opportunities be fostered if this means sacrificing freedoms. The order is strict: 1, 2 and 3. Improving 2 and 3 but worsening 1, or improving 3 at the cost of worsening 2, is unacceptable.

Public freedoms, then, have notable priority in Rawls's theory of justice as fairness. The public freedoms his theory designates are political freedom (the right to vote and occupy public positions), the right to expression and assembly, the rights of conscience and thought, personal rights (including protection against psychological and physical aggression), the right to protection against arbitrary arrest, and the right of personal property. With regard to the final right, Rawls (1996) unequivocally states that private ownership of the means of production is not fixed at the level of the first principles of justice.

One of the interesting implications of Rawls's theory of justice is that it is concerned about people's responsibility in making their choices. It does not make people responsible for circumstances they have not chosen. It seems logical to me to make an individual responsible for having very expensive tastes – like collecting sports cars – and difficult to accept that society should have to compensate this person for any effects arising from a preference that is way above the average in terms of price.

Again, I believe it is very reasonable not to make another individual responsible for being blind or paralysed from birth, and hence it is easier to accept that society should compensate for such major handicaps that this person is in no way responsible for, although the precise way of doing so is more difficult to agree upon.

Rawls recognises that equality of resources seems to be an equitable idea for many people. Yet we still need to know what resources we are referring to. We can establish a distinction between social resources and natural resources, which would give us a packet of primary social goods and another of primary natural goods. Within the first packet we could include those goods that are distributed by the social institutions, as in the cases of income, opportunities, rights and freedoms. In the second packet we have intelligence, health, natural aptitudes, physical resources and so on, which, although they might be affected by the social institutions, are not directly distributed by them.

The justification of Basic Income, starting out from this normative theory, can be constructed as follows. One must recall that under the leximin stipulation of respect, first, for formal freedoms and, second, fair equality of opportunities, one must choose the situation that best satisfies the maximin criterion. Hence, according to Rawls, inequalities of economic or social advantages are not justified if formal freedoms and equality of opportunity are jeopardised in any way. Under such criteria, one might quite quickly be able to justify an income for the least privileged to the maximum economically sustainable level. However, it is still necessary to justify the affirmation that this income should be a Basic Income. Why Basic Income and not some other kind of conditioned subsidy? In order to justify Basic Income we shall have to start by recalling something I have mentioned earlier: the importance of self-respect as a primary, and perhaps the principal, good according to Rawls. If we take this crucial primary good as our starting point, Basic Income can be justified from the theory of justice as fairness, and few steps are needed to achieve this.

Conditioned subsidies in our societies single out people who cannot satisfy their most elementary or basic needs. The social services systems are humiliating, as many authors have shown. These systems clearly distinguish between those who can and those who cannot support themselves. Many possible beneficiaries of these conditioned or means-tested subsidies do not ask for them because of the humiliating conditions imposed. With regard to the primary good of self-respect, Basic Income would seem to be better than any conditioned subsidy. I shall discuss some of the major problems associated with these subsidies in Chapter 6, but for the moment I am only concerned to highlight their relationship with self-respect. This interpretation of justice as fairness (to repeat, this is not Rawls's own interpretation), on the basis of the importance given to self-respect, justifies Basic Income above any kind of conditioned subsidy. Without self-respect, one is as good as socially paralysed, for nothing seems worth doing, as Rawls states. In her text on the ethical attractions of the 'scandalous proposal' of Basic Income, Catriona McKinnon (2006: 1) expresses the matter as follows: 'Self-respect is a fundamental human good.'

2.3 THE REAL FREEDOM JUSTIFICATION: A REAL-LIBERTARIAN SOCIETY

The third and final normative justification of Basic Income that I shall present is Philippe Van Parijs's theory of real freedom. This is a theory of justice that, it is no exaggeration to state, was constructed in order to justify Basic Income. Van Parijs, in both solo and co-authored works, had for some years been advocating the need or appropriateness of Basic Income before elaborating his real-freedom theory of justice as a thoroughgoing defence of it. *Real Freedom for All* (1995) is Van Parijs's 'life work' and he notes in the Preface that he began work on the book in 1977, 18 years before it was published.

Van Parijs says that his theory of justice is 'authentically liberal' or 'real freedom for all'. He starts out from two basic convictions. First, capitalist societies are replete with huge and indefensible inequalities and, second, liberty is of prime importance. A free society, for Van Parijs, is one that satisfies three conditions or principles: (1) that there is a well-defended system of rights (security); (2) that within this structure each person is owner of himself or herself (ownership of self); and (3) that within this structure each person has the greatest possible degree of opportunity for doing whatever he or she might like to do (leximin order of opportunity).

This third condition means that, in a free society, the person who has fewest opportunities will not have fewer than the person who has fewest opportunities in any other social arrangement we can hypothesise. If the opportunities available to those in the least favourable positions in the society in question are equal, then the society may be judged in terms of the two people on the next level up, and if this results in another draw, those of the next two people up, and so on. This is the lexicographic order, which I have already defined.

A society that satisfied these three conditions would be a really free society. The difference between really free and formally free resides in the third condition. A formally free society meets the first two conditions but not the third. For example, if I accept paid work that is really undesirable (very badly paid, or extremely boring, or disagreeable, or a bit of everything) because I have no other option but to accept prospects that are even worse, I am not taking this job freely. I am obliged to take it. Formally, I am free to accept the job or not. Formal freedom is conditional in a very precise sense: without resources it cannot be real. Real freedom includes formal freedom but has the additional requirement of resources. If I am to be able to go on a journey I need to be free to cross the borders of my country or state (formal freedom) and to have the resources to be able to do it (real freedom). The third condition to which I allude speaks of 'opportunities' precisely in the sense that this example suggests. There is evident similarity between this conception and that of Amartya Sen. Freedom, for Sen, is about the real opportunity to be able to engage in what we value.

Now that we have elaborated a little on the three conditions for a really free society, we are left with a question. What order must be established between these three conditions and which one has to prevail over the others? A free society should prioritise the first condition over the second and the second over the third. Security would be the primary condition and ownership of oneself would take precedence over ordering opportunities in favour of the worst-situated members of society. Van Parijs (1995: 26) says that this order of priorities should be applied with a light hand, which is to say that he 'does not propose a rigid lexicographic approach'. To more practical effects, this light-handed approach to preferences among the three conditions means that small infractions of law and order might be tolerated if trying to avoid them would seriously jeopardise self-ownership. Imagine that, in order to avoid robberies (in other words, to avoid something that is a direct assault on the first condition, one's own security) we would have to construct an immense police state. Van Parijs considers that the costs this would suppose (in a sense going beyond the strictly economic one) would not compensate for a possible decrease in the incidence of robberies.

The third condition (where, to repeat, every person has the maximum possible opportunity to do whatever he or she might wish to do) uses the expression 'might wish to do', which may seem rather odd, so here I should elaborate a little on Van Parijs's idea. He starts with the traditional distinctions between positive and negative freedom,[9] which have sometimes been simplified into a distinction between freedom *to* and freedom *from*. Van Parijs is of the view that freedom as individual sovereignty is at once 'freedom to' and 'freedom from'. So, when I can do what I want, am I free? Van Parijs would say not necessarily. If freedom consists in not facing any obstacle to doing what I wish, then any adept manipulation of my preferences, either through the actions of others or my own desire, can adapt what I want to what I have. The possibility of increased conformity in a person whose preferences have been manipulated through either of these variants should not be overlooked. To assert that a person increases his or her freedom through such manipulation is, as Van Parijs says, somewhat counterintuitive. This is the story of the 'contented slave'. In effect, nobody denies the possibility that a slave can be happy (for whatever reason, including the possibility that he wants what he has because of kinky personal preferences), but few would be ready to declare that this means greater freedom.

The problem suggested by the 'contented slave' refers us to many situations in which people in a position that is deemed to be unjust from the standpoint of several plausible and not particularly strict criteria of justice might consider their position to be just because of a set of factors that are summarised in what I have called 'manipulation of preferences'. We could include here conditions such as the Stockholm syndrome, the case of women who accept their condition of dependence or subordination, or labourers who see their grim conditions of work as something inevitable. Van Parijs gets around the 'contented slave' problem by stipulating that being free does not consist in not being prevented from doing exactly what one likes but, 'in not being prevented from doing not just what one wants to do, but whatever one *might like* to do' (Van Parijs, 1995: 19). In this view, no manipulation of preferences, whether by the slaves themselves or by anyone else, can make a society of contented slaves 'any freer than an otherwise identical society' (ibid). Van Parijs goes on to say that this leads to a distinction between a society whose members are prevented from carrying out what they all wish to do and another whose members are prevented from doing something that nobody could seriously want to do.

I have now reached the point where I can bring Basic Income into the theory of real freedom for all. And through the front door at that. A free society that honours the three principles defined by Van Parijs must have a set of institutions to make them possible. Hence, the first principle, security, requires a solid structure of rights. The second, self-ownership, requires clear autonomy, which is the same as saying that, within the structure of these rights, each person has individual sovereignty. As for the third principle, the leximin order of the set of opportunities comes down to a perception of Basic Income, which would be the most significant institutional consequence of the conception of real freedom. Effectively, if real freedom makes special mention of means and not only of rights, people's income becomes a very important factor. We are not merely referring to the freedom to consume but, as I have stated, to the freedom to live as one might like to.

The definition of Basic Income offered by Van Parijs (1995: 35) is very similar to the one I have given in Chapter 1. To be precise, he says, that this is an income paid by the government to each accredited member of society (1) even if he or she does not want to work, (2) without regard for whether he or she is rich or poor, (3) without regard to cohabitation arrangements, and (4) independently of the part of the country in which he or she lives.[10]

The stipulation of being a full member of society includes a period of legal residence, which is to say that the Basic Income offered would not be restricted to the citizens of that country. Nonetheless, immigration laws themselves are something that, strictly speaking, the Basic Income proposal does not include, since political positions with regard to these laws arise from other social motivations. Nonetheless I should say in passing, although I shall discuss this at greater length in Chapter 9, that a universal Basic Income could be a viable response (and certainly more humane and just than building evermore sophisticated fences, and passing evermore draconian laws, not to mention whipping up xenophobia) to the issue of how to respond to uncontrolled immigration into Western Europe (the so-called 'human avalanche') and the social conditions that give rise to it.

And now for another turn of the screw to Van Parijs's defence of Basic Income. So far we have not taken the so-called internal endowments into account (intelligence, other kinds of attractiveness or natural defects). We are not all equally equipped or equally under-equipped by the lottery of nature. Some people are healthy and athletic and others are sickly; some are very intelligent (though I need not specify here what I understand by intelligence or types of intelligence) and others are slow-witted; some are highly sexually attractive and others are even repulsive; some enjoy impeccable physical functioning of their bodies while others suffer from serious impediments affecting part or the whole of their bodies. And so on. Van Parijs considers that anyone who suffers from some kind of disability, whatever it is and taking the term in a very broad sense, will not enjoy the same opportunities to do what he or she might like to be able to do as somebody who has been physically blessed in the natural lottery. He believes that the former should be allocated more external resources than the latter. Here he uses the criterion of 'undominated diversity', a concept coined by Bruce

Ackerman (1993). The idea of undominated diversity attempts precisely to capture the problem of internal endowments. The internal endowments of X 'dominate' (can be seen as more valuable than) the internal endowments of Z if and only if every individual, given his or her conception of a good life, would prefer X's endowments to Z's.

What is the idea behind this apparently convoluted criterion? Let us imagine that Montserrat is an intelligent, attractive and cultured woman and that Anastasia is not excessively intelligent and she has little education but that, in athletic terms, she is far superior to Montserrat. Let us also suppose that this is the end of the story, that there is nothing else to compare. Montserrat's internal endowments do not completely dominate Anastasia's. Of the four endowments we have imagined, Montserrat is way ahead of Anastasia in three but way behind in one. This example now enables me to raise a problem. If we do not take conceptions of a good life into account, dominance could only occur when Montserrat is superior to Anastasia in all respects. The problem rapidly emerges. It would be very difficult, then, for undominated diversity to occur. If we expand the endowments to be compared and if Montserrat is ahead of Anastasia in all four aspects I have mentioned, Anastasia could still have more beautiful eyes than Montserrat. In Ackerman's view, once the internal endowments of two people have been compared, there are only two possible conclusions. The first is that one person dominates (in internal endowments) another, who might then ask for assistance to compensate for this dominance. The second conclusion is that there is no dominance and, in such a case, no compensation can be demanded.

Although we can say at this point that Basic Income is justified in terms of the theory of real freedom for all as long as security and autonomy are respected along with the criterion of undominated diversity, I should like to mention the role that Van

Parijs assigns to jobs before concluding my discussion of his work. He considers that in late twentieth-century and early twenty-first-century capitalism, where there is a scarcity of jobs, people who have jobs appropriate a greater share of the available employment opportunities than is due to them. Every person who is able to work, who wishes to work but who cannot find a job should ideally have an equal share in the total of remunerated work available. If there were full employment or voluntary unemployment, Van Parijs's idea would still hold because there are a lot of jobs that are disagreeable for many reasons, or that people simply do not want. Basic Income, in his view, would be a way of bringing about a redistribution of the real freedom that is being enjoyed by those who are unjustifiably appropriating the limited opportunities to engage in remunerated work.

2.4 LIBERAL THEORIES AND REPUBLICAN THEORIES

I have now offered normative justifications of Basic Income from the standpoints of three different theories of justice. There is little doubt that the third, Van Parijs's theory of real freedom, is the one that is most directly elaborated for the endeavour of justifying Basic Income. What these theories have in common is that they define themselves as liberal. While it is true that there are notable variations among them (as there are between them and other theories I have not discussed here), differences as great as we might find between Freidrich Hayek, John Rawls or Nozick-style libertarians, what they do have in common is the fact that they share a standpoint that 'precludes any kind of hierarchy of the different conceptions of the good life that might be found in society' (Van Parijs, 1991: 244). At this point, some clarifications are needed.

The first is concerned with the word 'liberalism', which may be subject to a great number of distinctions, divisions and subdivisions. Examples include property-based liberalism and solidarity-based (or egalitarian) liberalism, and then we have economic liberalism and political liberalism. These subdivisions are of no special interest here. What is interesting is the distinction I believe is fundamental: that between political liberalism and academic liberalism. The former, which has been in existence for no longer than two centuries, is the liberalism that prevailed through the nineteenth and twentieth centuries and the present century so far. It is up to historians to continue analysing its role and its enduring enmity towards democracy, freedom and equality.[11] Academic liberalism, however, is an amalgam in which we find writers on the right of the political spectrum, others in the centre and still others on the more or less moderate left. The three theories of justice I have discussed are just a sample of the great differences that exist between the different varieties of what I call academic liberalism.

With my next chapter in mind, I think it is also interesting to look for a moment at some 'truths' that are repeated *ad nauseum*, supposedly to mark the differences between liberal and republican theories of justice. In brief, according to the caricature, academic liberalism is not concerned with virtue so it is not a morally perfectionist doctrine and therefore it can have a neutral conception of the state. Thus, the story goes, academic liberalism is a non-sectarian political doctrine that fosters tolerance. It symmetrically follows, in this line of thinking, that republicanism (I shall discuss its diversity in Chapter 3 but, for the moment, I am only concerned with the caricature that unites all its manifestations) is concerned about the virtue of citizens, so it is morally perfectionist and therefore it is incompatible with a state that is neutral with regard to the different conceptions of what is good.[12]

This inanity, in its different, more or less sophisticated versions, can be found in a great number of academic books and articles, and can be heard in many universities around the world, the Anglo-Saxon world in particular. Is there any truth in this? The short answer is no. I shall discuss this endlessly parroted cliché at greater length in my next chapter, which is concerned with presenting, without further distractions, the republican justification for Basic Income.

3 THE NORMATIVE REPUBLICAN JUSTIFICATION

[U]tinam tam facile vera invenire possim falsa convincere (If only it was as easy to reveal the truth as to demonstrate the falsehood).

Marcus Tullius Cicero (106–43 BC), 44 BC

What is republicanism? How might republicanism justify Basic Income? These two questions are not difficult to answer, and addressing them gives me the chance to raise some important philosophical (not to mention social and political) issues.

Philip Pettit, one of the authors who has done most in the Anglo-Saxon world to revitalise republicanism, describes it (1997) as having its origins in classical Rome, a resurgence in the Renaissance (from the fourteenth through to the sixteenth century) and particular prominence in the Dutch Republic (1588–1795), the years of the English Civil War (1642–51) and, finally, in the period that culminated in the American (1775–83) and French (1789–94) revolutions. I think we should look further in seeking the origins of republicanism, especially if we are to understand the feature that is of greatest import here: its democratic-plebeian aspect. This takes us back to the Athenian democracy of 25 centuries ago (507–321 BC) and to the republic that I shall sketch in Section 3.1.

Unlike real-world liberalism, which only goes back to the early nineteenth century (in fact, the word 'liberalism' was coined in 1812 by the *Cortes de Cádiz* – the Spanish government in exile in Cádiz – after which the term spread around the globe), republicanism has a 2000-year-long tradition that developed in the ancient Mediterranean world. Some names that are associated with republicanism are (in its plebeian-democratic version), Ephialtes (?–461 BC), Pericles (495–429 BC), Protagoras (485–411 BC) and Democritus (470/460–370/360 BC), and (in the anti-democratic or oligarchic version) Aristotle (384–322 BC) and Cicero (106–43 BC). These two great variants of republicanism also appear in the modern world. Democracy aspires to the universalisation of republican freedom and hence to the inclusion as citizens, and even as members of government, of the poor majority. The anti-democratic version would exclude from civil and political life all those who live from their own labour, while aspiring to a monopoly of political power by rich proprietors. Some names we should associate with the modern renaissance of republicanism are Marsiglio of Padua (?–1342), Machiavelli (1469–1527), (some of) Montesquieu (1689–1755), John Locke (1632–1704), Rousseau (1712–1778), Kant (1724–1804), Adam Smith (1723–1790), Thomas Jefferson (1743–1826), James Madison (1751–1836), Robespierre (1758–1794) and Marx (1818–1883).

In focusing on what I understand to be the most decisive contributions of republicans from different periods, my aims are twofold. First, I shall single out from a historical perspective the most relevant aspects of the republican conception of freedom, thereby constructing an evolutionist – certainly not creationist – declaration of freedom. I am not 'creating' a concept of freedom in order to discuss it, but rather attending to the main features of this republican concept of freedom as it has been understood by some of its most outstanding representatives over different epochs. Second, I shall end the chapter by providing a solid republican foundation for Basic Income.

3.1 ARISTOTLE: MATERIAL EXISTENCE AS A CONDITION OF FREEDOM

One of the outstanding historians of the classical world, G.E.M. de Ste. Croix (1910–2000), accurately described Aristotle as the great political sociologist of ancient Greece:

> Far from being an anachronistic aberration confined to Marx and his followers, the concept of economic class as the basic factor in the differentiation of Greek society and the definition of its political divisions turns out to correspond remarkably well with the view taken by the Greeks themselves; and Aristotle, the great expert on the sociology and politics of the Greek city, always proceeds on the basis of class analysis and takes it for granted that men will act, politically and otherwise, above all according to their economic position.
>
> (Ste. Croix, 1981: 79)

No less important among Aristotle's contributions was his concept of freedom. In order to elucidate this, I shall need to give some idea of the society that Aristotle was writing about.

Aristotle lived during the final period of the great Athenian democracy, which lasted from 507 BC to 322/321 BC. This long period of 185 years saw only two attempts to restore oligarchy, in 411 and 404–03. Coinciding almost exactly with the death of Aristotle, one of the momentous transformations that took place in Athens during the democracy, was the result of the reforms of Ephialtes in 462–61 BC. With these came the gradual introduction of payment for undertaking political tasks, first for jury service and participating in the Council (*Boulé*) that prepared the matters that were to be discussed in the Assembly (*Ekklesia*) and, somewhat later, in 403 BC, for participating in the Assembly itself. The payment, which was less than an artisan's salary, did not amount to much but it did permit the poorest citizens to have an effective role in the political life of the city if they so wished.[1] Ephialtes' reforms meant:

> the invasion of political life by the poor demos and, in fact, with the exception of two coup attempts by the oligarchy, Athens was a republic that was governed without interruption for 140 years by the democratic party of the poor.[2]

This is the period, the closing years of the Athenian democracy, in which Aristotle lived and of which he was an acute, and indisputably even-handed, critic. His political works, especially *Politics*, cannot be understood unless this background is taken into account. Although Aristotle frequently expressed his concern (unwarranted, given the magnanimity of the democracy at this point) over the danger of the 'excesses' of 'extreme' democracy, in particular possible expropriation of the wealth of the great proprietors, the democracy was very indulgent with the rich. In times of war, it is true, they had to pay the *eisphora*, a tax levied to help cover the republic's war expenses. This was, however, a long way from being any kind of appropriation.

Apart from the rich and the poor, Aristotle sometimes cited the *hoi mesoi*, men of moderate wealth who might be described as 'middle class' today, although normally he stuck to his dichotomy of rich and poor, by which he meant proprietors and men who possessed nothing or almost nothing (*hoi aporoi*). Aristotle considered that the economic situation of a man was the decisive factor that conditioned his political activity. This idea appears insistently in his writings on more directly social concerns, although he did not argue it directly but rather took it for granted since it was so widely accepted in his world. It is worth mentioning in passing that a great number of other writers have shared this class-based view of politics over the centuries.[3] It was only around the middle of the twentieth century that academics turned their backs on this relationship between economic situation and political behaviour.

For Aristotle (and for many others, for example Plato), there is no doubt that the class that takes power, whether rich or poor, will govern for its own benefit. 'For tyranny is a kind of monarchy which has in view the interest of the monarch only; oligarchy has in view the interest of the wealthy; democracy, of the needy: none of them the common good of all' (*Politics*, 3.7, 1279b, 5).[4] He says that, 'Oligarchy is based on the notion that those who are unequal in one respect are in all respects unequal; being unequal, that is, in property, they suppose themselves to be unequal absolutely' (*Politics*, 1301a, 31–33), and remarks that, 'the very rich think it unfair that the very poor should have an equal share in government as themselves' (*Politics*, 1316b, 1–3).

The importance Aristotle gives to the rich–poor divide is crucial. Rich and poor comprise the main part of the polity. He says:

> But the same persons cannot be poor and rich at the same time. For this reason the rich and the poor are especially regarded as parts of a state. Again, because the rich are generally few in number, while the poor are many, they may appear to be antagonistic, and as one or the other prevails they form the government. Hence

arises the common opinion that there are two kinds of
government – democracy and oligarchy.

(*Politics*, 1291b, 8–13)

What does Aristotle understand by 'the poor'? The answer has
little to do with the way we understand these words at the
beginning of the twenty-first century. Although I shall elaborate
on some of the different aspects of poverty in Chapter 5, for the
moment I shall only note that nowadays we associate 'the poor'
with those who fall below some kind of more or less arbitrary
statistical criterion. This might be, for instance, an income of
less than 50 or 60 per cent of the per capita average for a particular zone, or less than US$2 per day in a specific territory or, to
give a final example, less than the amount of money that some
government ministry designates as being the minimum required
in order to live.

Again, in a very different way, Aristotle distinguished
between poor freemen and slaves. We cannot dwell on slaves
here because this would be to stray too far from my main line
of argument. In brief they were, for Aristotle, little more than
walking, talking instruments that had no part in civil society. In
speaking of poor freemen, Aristotle, like his contemporaries, is
referring to all non-enslaved men with no property (poverty-
stricken peasants with barely enough land to sustain a family,
day labourers, builders, painters, sculptors, quarry workers,
foundry workers, dyers, silversmiths, marble cutters, decora-
tors, engravers, cart drivers, postillions, rope-makers, tanners,
road workers and others). These poor freemen lived from their
own labour and depended on others – the proprietors – in order
to be able to engage in their different kinds of work. Their very
existence was in the hands of the rich.

For Aristotle, the rich were proprietors, people whose material existence was guaranteed precisely thanks to their property.

The most important kind of property in antiquity, and for many centuries afterwards, was land. The class of proprietors consisted of people who hired others to ensure their supply of the needs (and luxuries) of the good life. In the period that concerns us here, the ratio between non-proprietor citizens and proprietor citizens was four to three. At this time, adult freemen accounted for 35,000 of the inhabitants of Athens. Of these, 20,000 were non-proprietors and 15,000 were proprietors. The lower levels of the bourgeoisie – humble artisans who earned a living without apprentices – were also regarded as non-proprietors. The crucial point is not so much the amount of wealth one had but the material possibility of not having to depend on anyone else in order to live. The rich, some much wealthier than others, did have their material existence guaranteed.

Government by the rich is oligarchy while government by the poor is democracy. 'For the real difference between democracy and oligarchy is poverty and wealth. Wherever men rule by reason of their wealth, whether they be few or many, that is an oligarchy, and where the poor rule, that is a democracy' (*Politics*, 1279b: 39; 1280a: 1–3). What makes a regime oligarchic or democratic is not a simple question of majority but one of class (the distinction between rich and poor, proprietors and free non-proprietors).

Aristotle, as I have noted, was no fan of Athenian democracy. For him, the poor free man (*phaulos*) does not have his material existence guaranteed because he has no property and for this very reason he cannot be free because, in not having this 'autonomous base of existence' (Bertomeu and Domènech, 2005: 37), he depends on another or others in order to live. And it makes no sense, he pronounces, to give full political rights to people who are not free. It should be remarked that the Athenian democrats had no quarrel (and neither did democratic republicans centuries later) with Aristotle's basic reasoning but, as democrats, they wanted to extend (universalise) political rights based on a guaranteed material existence to the population as a whole. They considered that political participation by poor freemen could be made possible with the *misthon*, the remuneration that was created with Ephialtes' reforms for performing specific tasks in the public sphere. Without this public remuneration they would never have been able to participate in democratic decision making. Hence we find Aristotle's opposition to the *misthon* and his counter-proposal of penalising the rich with fines when they did not attend public assemblies.

Aristotle perfectly captures the role of the *misthon* as a substitute for property (a very important republican idea to which I shall return, in Section 3.6, when I discuss Basic Income as universalisation of property) that could enable the autonomous material existence of the poor. However, this is Aristotle the *Realpolitker*, a side of him I shall not explore. The key question, to which I shall return below, is this: for Aristotle, the man who does not have a guaranteed material existence cannot be free because he necessarily depends on another or others in order to live.

3.2 PROPERTY IN CICERO

The Roman world was fervently concerned with status. And what gives status is wealth. As Ste. Croix notes, 'Ovid put it beautifully in three words: *dat census honoures*, "it is property that confers rank" (Amores III. Viii. 55)' (1981: 425). Roman *ius civile* is a monument of intellectual rigour that meticulously regulated all kinds of personal and family relations, but if one question merits special attention it is property rights, a particularly sacred matter for the Roman ruling classes, as Ste. Croix emphasises. I shall illustrate this by way of the veritable obsession of Cicero, another great (indubitably oligarchic) republican, with the inviolability that he considered property rights must have. First, however, I shall look briefly at a particular contractual distinction in Roman law in order to demonstrate that, in the Roman conception of republican freedom, a person who did not have the material means of existence guaranteed and who therefore depended on another or others in order to live, was in a situation that was the very negation of freedom.

This is a distinction between two kinds of work contract: the *locatio conductio opera* and the *locatio conductio operarum*. With the former, one person contracted another (for example, a silversmith) to do the job specified in the contract. The second was a contract for services whereby one person engaged another so that, for a certain period of time, the latter would do all the jobs he was told to do. The second contract was deemed degrading because it undermined freedom, while the first was seen as being perfectly dignified because it concerned a specific service supplied by someone in a certain category (let us say a dyer or a tanner). It was a contract agreed to between free men. If the *locatio conductio operarum* is considered unworthy of free men it is because one person becomes dependent on another and hence it is freedom that is at stake. For Cicero, in his *De Officiis* (On Obligations), making one's labour power available for exploitation on such general terms in exchange for a salary is the same as entering into a bond of servitude, and this is almost identical to what Aristotle had called 'limited slavery' two centuries earlier.[5]

Cicero is a key thinker for any in-depth understanding of oligarchic republicanism. More than 2000 years before the philosophical champions of libertarianism (see Section 2.1 above) appeared, he revealed an overriding concern with the inviolability of property rights (the first in a long line of thinkers, as Ste. Croix notes (1981: 286)). In Cicero's own words, 'The man in an administrative office ... must make it his first care that everyone shall have what belongs to him and that private citizens suffer no invasion of their property rights by act of the state' (*De Officiis*, Book II, Chapter XXI). The statesman's concern for preserving property must be duly accompanied by his refraining from any impulse to redistribute it because 'what more ruinous policy than that could be conceived? For the chief purpose of the establishment of the constitutional state and municipal governments was that individual property rights might be secured.' Cicero was in no doubt that harmony would be destroyed:

> when money is taken away from one party and bestowed upon another; and, second, they do away with equity, which is utterly subverted, if the rights of property are not respected. For, as I said above, it is the peculiar function of the state and the city to guarantee to every man the free and undisturbed control of his own particular property.[6]
>
> (*De Officiis*, Book II, Chapter XXII)

Hand-in-hand with Cicero's oligarchic republicanism goes an undisguised contempt for the working classes. This owner of one of Rome's great fortunes, 'in whom we can often find the choicest expression of any given kind of Roman hypocrisy' (Ste. Croix, 1981: 331), says quite unashamedly that:

> Unbecoming to a gentleman, too, and vulgar are the means of livelihood of all hired workmen whom we pay for mere manual labour, not for artistic skill; for in their case the very wage they receive is a pledge of their slavery.
>
> (*De Officiis*, Book I, Chapter XLII)

A little further on, he adds:

[56]

Least respectable of all are those trades which cater for sensual pleasures:
>   'Fishmongers, butchers, cooks, and poulterers,
>   And fishermen,'

as Terence says, 'Add to these, if you please, the perfumers, dancers, and the whole *corps de ballet*.'

There are many more apposite quotes from different early anti-democratic or oligarchic republicans but let us now take a leap of 1800 years to a democratic republican whose thought would continue to be incontrovertibly influential in posterity.

3.3 THE RIGHT OF EXISTENCE: ROBESPIERRE

If any author was derided and slandered immediately after his death, it was Maximilien Robespierre (1758–1794). This might be expected from right-wing intellectuals, politicians and propagandists, and is even predictable. That the left should not have been much more sympathetic towards this politician and thinker is rather surprising.[7]

Robespierre was the key figure of the French Revolution. Upon his death the revolution quickly took a reactionary turn that would soon afterwards culminate in the Napoleonic Empire. What concerns us most here, however, is the contribution of this revolutionary as a republican. While his works and speeches amount to ten volumes (published after 1910), I shall focus only on the parts discussing property, inequalities, freedom and social existence.[8]

Though only in passing, it is worth mentioning that for Robespierre, as for Aristotle, the two most important parts of the polity are the rich and the poor. Some 2100 years after Aristotle's pronouncement, Robespierre uses very similar terms in a speech of 2 February 1790: 'France is unquestionably divided into two parts, the people and the aristocracy.'

What is property for Robespierre? In a speech he gave before the Convention on 24 April 1793 he reflects at length upon the matter:

> Ask the trader in human flesh what property is. He will tell you, showing you a coffin, which he calls a boat, where he has boxed up and branded men who seem to be alive: 'These men are my property for I have paid for them at so much per head'. Ask this gentleman, who has lands and vassals, or this one who believes that the world is shattered because he no longer has them. He will give you almost the same ideas about property. Ask the august members of the Capetian dynasty and they will tell you that the most sacred of all property is indisputably hereditary right, which they have enjoyed since ancient times, the right to oppress, debase, and legally suffocate, as monarchs, and at their whim, the 25 million inhabitants of the territory of France.

This stark description of property prepares us for what Robespierre then offered as a normative view in which he states what property must be in order to be socially just. He summarises this in the form of articles in the same speech.

Article 1. Property is the right of every citizen to enjoy and dispose of the portion of goods that is guaranteed by law.
Article 2. The right to property is limited, as are all other rights, by the obligation to respect the rights of others.
Article 3. Property cannot jeopardise the security, liberty, existence or property of others.

Article 4. Any possession or any kind of commerce that violates
this principle is illicit and immoral.

Property, for Robespierre, must be limited and must not jeopardise freedom or existence. If property does not comply with at
least these two requisites, it is illicit and immoral. In his speech
to the Convention of 2 December 1792, he asks, 'Why should
not the laws detain the homicidal hand of the monopolist just as
they do with the common murderer?'

Property and freedom are intimately related. Addressing the
deputies, Robespierre says:

> In defining liberty as the foremost of man's goods, as the
> most sacred of the rights man inherits from nature, you
> have rightly said that its limits are constituted by the
> rights of others. Why have you not applied this principle
> to property, which is a social institution; as if the eternal
> laws of Nature were less inviolable than the conventions
> of men? Have you multiplied the articles to ensure
> greater freedom in the exercise of property and said noth-
> ing that determines its legitimate character?
>
> (Concerning the Declaration of the Rights
> of Man and of the Citizen, 24 April, 1793)

This insistence on the idea that not all property is legitimate
runs through Robespierre's work. If it threatens freedom, property is not legitimate. For Robespierre, at the root of the
destruction of freedom is great economic inequality, 'the source
of all evils'. In a speech of 5 April 1791, he scolds the legislators, 'you have done nothing for liberty if your laws do not aim
to diminish, by judicious and effective means, the extreme
inequality of fortunes.' He comes back to this on 24 April 1793
when he observes, 'Really, there was no need for a revolution in

order to explain to the world that extreme disproportion of wealth is the origin of many evils and many crimes.'

It is interesting, too, to note how, in a speech he made as early as April 1791, Robespierre was already pointing out that proprietors were not the only people who had the right to call themselves citizens. 'The rich ... have tried to ensure that only proprietors are worthy of the title of citizen. They have called their private interest general interest and, in order to succeed in their endeavour, have taken over all social powers'.

Almost as a summary of his deliberations on property, liberty and great social inequalities, Robespierre repeatedly demonstrates his deep conviction that society should guarantee the material existence of all citizens. There are many passages to cite on this and the most acute and abundant are from the last 18 months before he went to the guillotine, at the age of 36. He insists that a society that does not guarantee the material existence of its citizens is not a just society and it should therefore not continue. In the speech of 24 April 1793, he declares, 'Society is obliged to secure the subsistence of all its members.' He continues, 'Providing the necessary help against poverty is a duty of the rich towards the poor. It is incumbent upon the law to determine how this debt must be paid.' Since society and, sometimes more directly, governments are responsible for hunger, poverty and the dreadful conditions in which the poor live, '[t]he wretchedness of citizens is nothing other than the crime of governments' (speech of 10 May, 1793). If there is one deservedly oft-repeated quote, it must be the following from Robespierre's speech on subsistence of 2 December 1792:

What is the primary aim of society? It is to maintain the inalienable rights of man. What is the foremost of these rights? The right to exist. Therefore the first social law is that which guarantees to all members of society the means of existence; all others are subordinate to that; property was instituted and guaranteed only in order to cement that law; if property is held it is first of all to live. And it is not true that property can ever be in opposition to the subsistence of men.

This first social law according to Robespierre is crucial to our discussion of Basic Income.

Thus far, I have focused on three authors (Aristotle, Cicero and Robespierre[9]) because there are overwhelming, although different, reasons for regarding them as key thinkers in the republican tradition. There are others whose importance is by no means negligible,[10] but now it is time to recapitulate.

3.4   REPUBLICAN FREEDOM

Whatever the differences between Aristotle's and Cicero's oligarchic conception of republican freedom and Robespierre's democratic view, all of them conceive of the question of freedom in the same way. What makes the difference between them is the extension of this freedom and who is deemed worthy of it. Only the rich, say the oligarchic republicans. All citizens, say the democratic republicans.

Let us now contrast Robespierre's account of how great inequalities have fatal consequences for freedom with two fragments of speeches made only a few months after his death on 28 July 1794 at the hands of the Thermidorian reactionaries. The first comes from Boissy d'Anglas (1756–1826), a Thermidorian deputy who says:

We must be governed by the best; the best are the most educated and the most concerned to uphold the laws.

Now, apart from some exceptions, you will not find men like this except among those who enjoy the ownership of some property, who are committed to the country in which it is to be found, to the laws that protect it, to the tranquillity that preserves it, and they owe to this property and the comforts it offers the education that has made them able to discuss, with sagacity and precision, the advantages and disadvantages of the laws that determine the fate of our country. ... A country that is governed by proprietors belongs to the social order; [a democracy], one that is governed by non-proprietors belongs to the state of nature.

The second quote comes from another well-known Thermidorian, Dupont de Nemours (1739–1817):

It is evident that the proprietors, without whose permission nobody could find lodgings and maintenance in all the country, are citizens *par excellence*. They are the sovereigns by the grace of God and nature, their work, their investments and the work and investments of their forbears.[11]

Besides his political activity, Dupont de Nemours founded the company that would bear his name to the present day, now in the form of a giant chemicals and 'healthcare' multinational.

To synthesise, in republican terms, X is free in social life if:

1. He or she does not depend on any other person in order to live, which is the same as saying that X's social life is guaranteed if he or she has some kind of property that furnishes a reasonable level of subsistence.
2. Nobody can arbitrarily (in other words, illicitly or illegally)

interfere in the autonomous sphere of social existence (in the property) of X.

3. This also means that the republic can lawfully interfere in X's sphere of autonomous social existence as long as the republican citizen is in a political relationship of equality with all the other free citizens of the republic and is therefore equal before the law being applied, which he or she has equally codetermined with the other citizens, with equal possibilities of protesting against it and of codetermining a different law that abolishes the one presently being enforced by the government.

4. That any interference (from an individual, several people or the republic as a whole) in the sphere of X's private social existence that damages it to the point of making X lose his or her social autonomy, leaving him or her at the mercy of other parties, is illicit.

5. That the republic is obliged to interfere in the sphere of X's private social existence if this private sphere enables X successfully to dispute with the republic the right to define the public good: which is to say, the guarantee of republican freedom to all members of the polity.

6. Finally that X is secure in his or her civic-political freedom because of a – more or less extensive – hard core of *constitutive* (and not purely instrumental) rights that nobody can appropriate. Any attempt by X willingly to alienate (sell or give away) these rights would mean losing his or her standing as a free citizen.[12]

For the republican tradition (whether we are talking about Aristotle, Cicero or Robespierre, among many others) X's set of opportunities is clearly delimited by the property that enables him or her to lead an autonomous social existence. We are not talking about any old set of opportunities but the set deriving from property. Full citizenship is not possible without material independence or without some 'control' over the set of opportunities thus specified. Political freedom and the exercise of citizenship are incompatible with the relations of domination by which proprietors and the rich exert *dominium* over people who are not completely free and who are subject to all sorts of interference, whether in the sphere of domestic life or in the juridical relations pertaining to the civil sphere, for example work contracts or the buying and selling of material goods.

Herein lies the great divide between democratic republicans and oligarchic republicans. For the former, the political task is to design mechanisms that make this freedom possible, by making the material existence of all the citizens, of all the population, possible. For the latter, it has always been to exclude from active political life those who are not *sui iuris* (possessed of autonomous legal rights). They accordingly find it necessary to draw the line between 'passive' citizens and 'active' citizens. Kant, for example, took the view that people who are under the tutelage of other individuals do not have civil independence. Minors, women and servants do not have it because they cannot ensure their own existence in terms of sustenance and protection; neither do pieceworkers, or people who cannot put the product of their labour on sale in the public arena and must therefore depend on nothing more than private contracts or arrangements of temporary bondage that spring from the unilateral will of the exercise of *sui iuris*.[13]

To sum up, in the republican tradition, the independence conferred by property is not just a matter of private interest. On the contrary, it is of crucial political importance, both in terms of the exercise of freedom and in achieving republican self-government, because having a guaranteed material base of existence is indispensable for political independence and competence.

3.5 REPUBLICAN VIRTUE AND NEUTRALITY

I concluded Chapter 2 by raising a number of issues, one of which concerned republican virtue and neutrality. To be specific, since republicanism is concerned with the virtue of citizens, it is frequently alleged that it is therefore morally perfectionist and hence incompatible with a neutral state. By means of some strange kind of inferential glissando, it is then claimed that republicanism is a politically sectarian doctrine and intolerant when it comes to different conceptions of good. Now it is time to respond to this.

Let us start with virtue. The historical republican tradition has never (a-institutionally) approached the question of virtue as a mere psychological-moral problem. Even going back to Aristotle, discussion of virtue has always been accompanied by institutional considerations and reference to the social and material bases that make (or do not make) republican virtue possible. Naturally virtue has its psychological-moral aspects but, while taking these into account, republicanism has always insisted that only on the basis of socio-material existence can virtue appear. Aristotle, as we have seen, denies that the poor freeman has an autonomous base of material existence because he has no property. This absence of an autonomous base of existence prevents him from being free, which is why Aristotle would deny political rights to poor freemen.

This clearly implies, then, that republican virtue has nothing to do with moral perfectionism. Neither does it appeal to any conception of the good life in isolation from social institutions. On the contrary, the republican tradition affirms that when citizens have a material base for their autonomous social existence guaranteed by the republic, they can develop the capacity of self-government in their private lives. Moreover, this facilitates further capacity for public activity. Evidently, this material base will mean that some citizens will stuff themselves with beer and cholesterol-laden food as they watch the most despicable programmes television serves up. Upholders of republicanism do not deny such an eventuality. What they do assert is that this material base offers the possibility (to a much greater degree than could occur without a guaranteed material existence) for an individual to grow in civic virtue, which is no more nor less – as I have said – than the ability to be self-governing in one's private life, thence to engage in public life in the full exercise of one's condition as a citizen or, in other words, as a materially independent citizen.

Let us now turn to the neutrality of the state. In academia, state neutrality is generally understood as the state not favouring one or other kind of good life. Conceptions of a good life must be a matter of personal choice. Academic liberal theories of justice are considered to be neutral with regard to different conceptions of the good life. Theories of justice that opted for defending and rewarding a specific form of the good life would be 'perfectionist'. I do not believe that the academic standpoint is very helpful, except in a few secondary matters. For the historical republican tradition, however, the really interesting point is different and we should first recall that, 'the thesis of state neutrality is a characteristically republican invention at least as old as Pericles' (Bertomeu and Domènech, 2006). As I understand it, what concerns historical republicanism is something that is much more suggestive and far-reaching than the standard views on state neutrality. While the state must obviously respect whatever different conceptions of the good life its citizens may embrace, it is also 'obliged' to interfere so as to destroy (or limit) the economic or institutional base of any person, business or private grouping that threatens successfully to dispute the republican state's right to determine what is in the public interest.

Let us imagine a private power that is so influential that it can impose its will (its conception of private good) on the state. This would mean that the state has de facto been stripped of its neutrality. It would also mean that a large part of the population (obviously depending on the case in question) is willy-nilly affected by this conception of private good. The republican conception of state neutrality consists precisely in the state's being able to intervene to prevent such an imposition. Two examples offered by Bertomeu and Domènech (2006) are sufficient to make this point very clear:

> [T]he Weimar Republic was fighting for the neutrality of the state when it fought, and eventually succumbed to, the great *Kartells* of German industry that financed Hitler's rise to power; the North-American republic was fighting – without success – for the neutrality of the state when it tried to rein in what Roosevelt called the 'economic monarchs' with the Antitrust Laws of 1937.

In his last book, *Making Globalization Work*, Joseph Stiglitz (2006: Chapter 7) notes that, much more recently, 41 companies contributed (to put it euphemistically) $150 million to US electoral campaigns between 1991 and 2001. These companies (amongst which are Microsoft, Disney and General Electric) were rewarded with tax relief amounting to $55,000 million in only three years! Stiglitz adds that, between 1998 and 2004, $759 million was paid out by big pharmaceutical companies to influence 1400 regulations being voted upon in the US Congress.

The problem of state neutrality for the republican tradition is not whether one should respect a conception of the good life that, for example, considers that it consists in repeated reading of H.P. Lovecraft's novels combined with almost uninterrupted listening to John Lennon, or whether such a conception should be protected by the state. It should of course be respected. The problem is whether, for example, the material existence of an individual or group of people depends on the investment plans of a transnational company; or whether the energy resources of a whole country should be at the disposition of the boards of directors of a handful of powerful companies; or whether the dogmas of some churches can lead to the expropriation of the conditions of material existence of any particular group of people.

3.6 THE REPUBLICAN JUSTIFICATION OF BASIC INCOME

The authors we have considered in the previous sections differ in many respects. We would also find many differences between republican writers whom we might have included but have not. Whatever their differences are, they share at least two convictions:

1. Being free means not having to depend on any other party in order to live and not being subject to arbitrary interference by any other party. Any person who does not have this 'right of existence' guaranteed because of a lack of property is not a citizen in his or her own right – *sui iuris* – but lives at the mercy of others and is not capable of cultivating or even exercising civic virtue because this dependence on another party subjects him or her to an alien regime – *alieni iuris* – thus making of him or her, to all intents and purposes, an 'alien'.
2. Republican freedom can extend to many (the plebeian democracy advocated by democratic republicans) or few (the plutocratic form of the oligarchic republicans), but it is always based on property and the material independence

deriving from that. This freedom cannot be sustained if property ownership is so unequal and so polarised in its distribution that a mere handful of individuals is in a position to challenge the republic, successfully overcoming any opposition from the citizenry so as to impose its own conception of the public good. When property is very unequally distributed, there is little if any space for the freedom of the remaining population, which has thus been deprived of it.[14]

Independence, material existence and the autonomous base (these expressions are perfectly interchangeable here) conferred by property constitute the indispensable condition for the exercise of freedom, as I have insisted. Hence the idea of republican upholders of Basic Income is to 'universalise property', which must be understood metaphorically. Nobody is seriously thinking of sharing out the lands and property of any given country, or the whole world, among the population in question. Universalising property in the republican sense must be understood as being equivalent to guaranteeing material existence (Casassas and Raventós, 2007).

The introduction of a Basic Income would suppose increased republican freedom, which is to say some enhanced degree of socioeconomic independence, or an autonomous base of existence that is much greater than what most of the world's citizens know today, especially the most vulnerable, most subjugated groups (a considerable number of wage workers, the poor in general and, in particular, in the poorest countries, the unemployed, women, and so on). I refer here to a set of people with the common feature of being susceptible to arbitrary interference by other groups or individuals. The personal and civic possibilities of such vulnerable groups would be greatly expanded by the republican freedom guaranteed by a Basic Income, as I shall argue below.

3.6.1 The material dependence of women

Women constitute a huge and heterogeneous group and, as we all well know, not all women are in the same social situation. Neither is it very disputable that a Basic Income would furnish a good many women with a degree of economic independence that they do not have at present.[15] Although Basic Income is, by definition, independent of any contribution that might be made in the sphere of labour, I believe I must stress here that, even while they receive no remuneration, most women work. I shall cover remunerated work in the market in some detail in Chapter 4 but this is only one among the existing kinds of work.

Among the republican arguments in favour of a Basic Income for women are:

- Basic Income offers a decisive response to the fact that social policy needs to adapt to changes in types of cohabitation, especially with regard to the increasing numbers of single-parent families headed by women.
- Since it is an individual allowance, Basic Income would improve the economic situation of many women who live with a partner – married or not – especially in the most impoverished sectors of society. At present, a considerable part of any means-tested subsidy is assigned to the family as a whole. Normally, the recipient is the head of the family – generally a man – so that family members in a weaker position – generally women – are deprived of access to and control over the use of this income. In Carol Pateman's view (2006: 115), 'A basic income is important for ... democratisation precisely because it is paid not to households but to *individuals as citizens*' [Pateman's emphasis].
- The economic independence that is afforded by Basic Income may become a kind of domestic 'counter-power'

that can modify the relations of domination and subordination between the sexes and increase the negotiating power of women in the household, especially those who are dependent on husbands or partners, or who receive a very low income from discontinuous or part-time jobs.

- As many feminist writers have shown over recent decades, the social security systems in rich countries operate on the assumption that women are economically dependent on their husbands. This means that any social security benefits obtained are a result of their husbands' tax contributions and not because of the women's standing as citizens. In the context of growing challenges to the stereotype of the male breadwinner, it would not be whimsical to suppose that any choices with regard to domestic labour could be made in a much more consensual form than what prevails at present.

Along with these four points, it is possible to engage in an even more comprehensive discussion of how Basic Income might favour the material existence of women in the republican sense, as Pateman points out. In brief, many of the problems related to reciprocity in political philosophy in recent years refer only to those activities that are directly related to remunerated work. Is reciprocity violated when a person receives an unconditional allowance – in this case a Basic Income – even when this person is perfectly able to engage in remunerated work and simply does not care to, as in the vociferously trotted-out case of the free-rider?[16] Pateman points out that this as a very limited way of approaching the problem because it only takes remunerated work into consideration. What is overlooked is the problem of reciprocity that arises in a very widespread non-remunerated type of work that is mostly carried out by women: domestic labour.

This brings us to an even more wide-ranging problem, which is one of the concerns of democratic republicanism. I refer to the historic – even after the abolition of the *ancien régime* – situation of dependence where women have perennially been subject to male domination. One example will help me to make my point. In 1792, Robespierre abolished the distinction between active and passive citizens, which is to say between those citizens that had the right to vote and those that did not, according to the amount of taxes they could pay. In other words, the active citizen enjoyed a certain level of wealth and the passive citizen had not attained this level. This refers exclusively to men. Women were excluded because of being dependents in the patriarchy.[17] This is where I can link up with the concern expressed by Pateman above. Basic Income, because of its universal scope, depending only on citizenship or accredited residence, is not allocated to homes or to people with specific characteristics (being men, for example) and it is therefore a means of offering an autonomous base to a considerable percentage of women who still depend on males (husbands, lovers, fathers, brothers or others) for their material existence.

3.6.2 The bargaining power of the working class and decommodification of labour

Let us look now at something to which a number of Basic Income supporters have referred with regard to the second vulnerable group, the working class: the decommodification of labour power.[18] In capitalist economies, people who do not own land or the means of production must sell their labour power on the job market to a proprietor of land or of some other means of production, otherwise known as the employer, in order to acquire the economic means that will permit their existence. This situation has been described as the commodification of labour power (or, more directly, commodification of work) because the capacity to work of people who do not have the property that would permit them to avoid this situation has become a commodity. Some workers may have their means of subsistence covered outside the market thanks to one or another mechanism of social provision. In this case, their labour power is decommodified. We might therefore speak of different degrees of commodification (or decommodification) of labour power. Basic Income would have a substantial effect on this as long as it was at least sufficient to permit 'the freedom not to be employed' (Pateman, 2006: 104).

Moreover, Basic Income would have another effect on the working class, one which from the republican perspective is particularly interesting, and this is enhanced bargaining power for workers vis-à-vis employers.[19] The security of income that the guarantee of Basic Income would offer would put hard-pressed workers in the position of not being obliged to accept a job under any conditions, however bad they might be. From the moment in which leaving the job market would seem practicable, this would mean a much more substantial negotiating position (or power of resistance, as it as sometimes been called) than workers have at present. If today's disgruntled workers take negotiations to breaking point, they do so knowing full well that proprietors can replace them by machines or by other unemployed workers – who fill the ranks of the so-called industrial reserve army ('relative surplus population', in Marx's words) – or that their subsistence directly and practically exclusively depends on the salary paid by the individuals on the other side of the negotiating table. The labour relationship under capitalism is extremely asymmetrical. The refuge of a regularly paid Basic Income would not only enable many workers to reject undesirable labour conditions convincingly and effectively but would also allow them to consider engaging in alternative forms of work that would permit them to aspire to higher levels of personal realisation.

A Basic Income would represent, in the case of a strike, a kind of unconditional and inexhaustible resistance fund. The consequences of this in terms of worker bargaining power are easy to imagine. If striking workers could count on a Basic Income they would be able to approach the option of going on strike in a much more secure fashion than at present when, depending on the duration of the strike, their salaries are docked, making their lives very difficult, to say the least, when there are no other sources of income within their reach. This is the situation of the immense majority of workers today.

To conclude, what I have tried to show in this chapter, using the contributions of a number of writers, is that the republican tradition is a particularly valuable programme of thought and action. The republican conception of freedom is highly exigent. Equality and liberty are not two variables for picking and choosing whether to have a bit more of one and a bit less of the other and vice-versa. Great social inequalities are the cause of lack of freedom. In a world such as ours at the beginning of the twenty-first century, where the private accumulation of vast fortunes coexists (frequently as a direct cause) with conditions of utter wretchedness, the freedom of hundreds of millions of people is seriously threatened even where it is not completely denied. In the socioeconomic conditions of this new century, Basic Income is nothing less than an institutional mechanism whereby it is possible to guarantee material existence to all citizens and accredited residents (of whatever territory). This would not be an inconsiderable achievement in today's world.

4 REMUNERATED WORK, DOMESTIC WORK AND VOLUNTARY WORK

> The bourgeois have very good grounds for falsely ascribing supernatural creative power to labour; since precisely from the fact that labour depends on nature it follows that the man who possesses no other property than his labour power must, in all conditions of society and culture, be the slave of other men who have made themselves the owners of the material conditions of labour. He can only work with their permission, hence live only with their permission.
>
> Karl Marx (1818–1883), 1875

Formulating a definition of work is a risky undertaking because one concept might be too narrow and another excessively broad and not very enlightening. Offering the definitions of some particularly interesting writers and then going on to discuss their respective advantages and disadvantages might shed some light on the matter, but this would be a diversion from my real interest here, which is Basic Income and its relationship with the three types into which I believe work can be classified. It is not my concern to defend a particular definition of work or attempt an in-depth analysis of the word. What I wish to do is to highlight those aspects of work that have a direct bearing on Basic Income and vice versa.

Until the late 1960s, 'work' was seen, in both academia and in everyday usage, as equivalent to a paid or remunerated job on the market. In other words, it was more or less strictly related to the production of goods and services. However, I understand work in a much broader sense, as that set of paid or unpaid activities whose results render goods and services for members of our species.[1] Apart from being closer to the real-world conditions of housewives, hunters and gatherers, and Fair Trade volunteer workers, for example, this is a useful definition because it enables me to include the three types of work in my classification below.

Though my definition is more encompassing than the salary-bound view of work, it does not imply that all activities can be classified as work. For example, I am in little doubt that introspection is an activity that can be almost heroic in some cases but it would not fit into this definition of work, and neither would pure ecstatic contemplation of beauty (animal, vegetable or mineral). Work should not simply be equated with effort either. Climbing a mountain of 3000 metres, having started out from an altitude of less than 2000 metres above sea level, certainly means considerable effort, but this cannot be classified as work. Neither shall I dwell on the distinction that needs to be made between the product or result of work and work itself. It is evident enough that shoes being turned out of a factory are the product of work, but not work itself. Hence the distinction between labour power and work, which can be particularly useful at times.

My definition does not require that work should be especially arduous. It may be autotelic, a particular kind of work or activity whose significance is not dependent upon something external to itself and that brings its reward in its own activities or execution. In fact, voluntary work, which I shall discuss below, is quite difficult to consider in anything but autotelic terms. However, most kinds of work are not autotelic but rather a necessity that must be endured. In the terms of my definition, work can be activities carried out almost solely in one's own interest. I might have a neighbour who loves making cakes for me. This may or may not be beneficial for me. The definition also permits us to infer that the result of an activity need not necessarily be some material object because it could be a service, remunerated or otherwise. Most results of domestic work, which I shall also discuss in some detail below, do not consist of material objects.

I should also stress that, as a methodological option, I have not mentioned any kind of social utility of work in my definition. The assumption here is that all work is useful for somebody or other. The political component of the idea of 'socially useful work' (and here the word 'political' enters the picture because opinions as to what does and what does not constitute socially useful work will depend on each individual's economic circumstances and social and ethical convictions) is enormous. For instance, the work of a lot of government employees, the military, top executives in big private companies, and a long list of others, may be considered by some people as completely useless if not out-and-out detrimental for society, besides being unnecessarily costly in some cases for taxpayers. Others may believe, in keeping with their political and social thinking, that such work is wholly useful. An oft-repeated example invoking the public good is 'national defence' or its present version of a 'war on terror', which provides a lot of clues as to the kind of political thinking of the person who proffers this example.[2]

In sum, what an individual might consider socially useful is problematic in both taxonomic and political terms. The fact that the definition of work I have used avoids this problem is, frankly speaking, one of its virtues. Moreover, the matter becomes exponentially more complicated if we attempt to establish a cardinal sequence instead of an ordinal sequence of 'socially useful work': for example how many times more useful is the work of somebody who works in a car-wash chain than that of a single mother at home looking after her two children, or how many times more useful is the work of a professor of Sanskrit than that of a monitor in a mountain-climbing course.[3]

4.1 THREE KINDS OF WORK

I believe that we can now proceed directly to my proposed classification of work. Wage labour constitutes a subset of remunerated jobs on the market. There are other remunerated kinds of work on the market that do not come under the heading of wage labour: for example the work done by freelancers. What I want to emphasise cannot be hedged about by a few technical distinctions. Remunerated work, in keeping with my previous stipulations, is a form of work. It is very important, there is no doubt about this, but it is only one form of work. The typology I shall employ in my account of how Basic Income and work are related is as follows: (1) remunerated work, (2) domestic work, and (3) voluntary work.[4]

Arguing that remunerated work is the only kind there is evidently means stipulating that other activities such as domestic and voluntary work are not truly work. Indeed, if remunerated work were the only activity to be exclusively accepted in a definition of 'work', this would lead to the unwarranted assertion that, in the economic space of the European Union only 40–45 per cent of the population would be 'working', from which one could infer that the remaining 55–60 per cent 'does not work'.

4.2 BASIC INCOME AND THE JOB MARKET

Remunerated work is sometimes called employment. Whatever words are used, the intention is only to encompass activities that give access to a source of income. Income may be a salary if the recipient is somebody with a job that depends on another person or persons, profit in the case of the owner of the means of production, payment if the person is self-employed and a pension for somebody who has retired from remunerated work activity. How the introduction of a Basic Income might affect remunerated work on the job market is a matter of particular interest and I believe that we can make some reasonable approximations to this. Any consideration of the effect on the job market of introducing a Basic Income (this depending on the amount of the Basic Income, as I shall discuss in Chapter 8) would have to keep in mind at least four points: (1) the incentives of waged work, (2) self-employment, (3) part-time paid work, and (4) pay rises in some jobs and pay cuts in others.

Incentives

In the case of incentives, the standard neoclassical economic model informs us that when real wages increase, two effects appear: the income effect and the substitution effect.[5] The latter effect would incline people to work more because the opportunity costs of leisure are now higher. In contrast, the income effect predisposes a person in precisely the opposite way because the increased salary tends to increase leisure time. This is because earning the same amount takes less time. Hence, only by combining the two effects can we see the final decision of the person in his or her choice between leisure and work. Obviously, if the substitution effect is greater than the income effect, the increase in real wages will be translated into a greater willingness to work. Analyses of the income effect on the offer of remunerated work start out from the hypothesis of free variation, as the individual prefers, of the number of working hours. The final result will be the combination of the person's preferences for more income or more leisure. In more technical terms, each person will try to maximise his or her utility in keeping with the budgetary restriction that will be determined by his or her wage level. In the case of a Basic Income being introduced, and bearing very much in mind its feature of being an income on the basis of which other income from different sources can be accumulated, all other factors being equal, it should be understood that people would have more opportunities to choose some kind of combination of the three kinds of work (remunerated, domestic and voluntary) than they do at present.

Suppose that Bautista receives a monthly salary of €960 as a waiter, working eight hours a day, the equivalent to €6 (net) per hour for 160 hours of work every month. One glorious day the government of his country decides to introduce a Basic Income of €430 per month. Assuming that his net income increases considerably, even though presumably Bautista will now have to pay more tax on his salary, his plans will almost undoubtedly change. The €430 will enable him to look for part-time work in return for, let's say, €500 a month. Imagine that he now decides to work an average of five hours a day, or 100 hours a month. In this new arrangement Bautista is only being paid €5 per hour but he also has three more hours every day that are free of dependent work, and he can use them for voluntary or domestic work, or enrol for some kind of training. This need not greatly affect his acquisitive power. Of course, Bautista's decisions will be conditioned by many factors such as his personal structure of preferences, his future projects and so on, but these do not affect our argument.

As for the possible consequences of the introduction of a Basic Income for the offer on the job market, the most analogous empirical studies come from the experience of Negative Income Tax (NIT). Between 1968 and 1980, NIT was introduced in four different areas of the United States and also in Manitoba, Canada. The American scheme known as SIME-DIME (Seattle-Denver Income Maintenance Experiment) is the longest lasting and most generous. The experiment covered 4800 people in the metropolitan areas of Seattle and Denver and its effects were greater on some groups than on others. Disincentives for wage work were greater among married white women and Hispanic men than in other groups, for example. The main conclusions that may be drawn from these experiments certainly call into question the most disturbing and doom-mongering predictions of non-experimental studies on the disincentives for wage labour that the introduction of certain types of subsidies supposedly entail, but this is about as much light as the NIT experiment can throw on the question of Basic Income.[6]

Another much more limited study (covering only 82 people) was carried out by Axel Marx and Hans Peeters (2004), this being a follow-up of people who had won in the Belgian Lottery (Win for Life), a monthly payment of €1000 for the rest of their days. The results, with all the limitations that the authors recognise, are worth mentioning because they shatter some widespread general preconceptions (along the lines of 'people would stop working') about the impact the introduction of a Basic Income might have on many people's attitudes to wage labour.[7] Another preconception shatterer is the study of Gamel et al (2006) on the impact of Basic Income on the propensity to work in France. In the words of Van der Veen and Van Parijs (2006: 4), '[The aim of Basic Income] is not, and its effect should not be, to reduce the proportion of people who participate in the labour market.'

Self-employment

There is little doubt that the introduction of a Basic Income could favour self-employment. As Ferry (1995) suggests, Basic Income would psychologically release the taste for risk. Again, it would markedly reduce the hazards of starting out in specific kinds of self-employment. Let us return to Bautista, the waiter who is paid €960 a month. A Basic Income of €430 a month is introduced. Let us assume that he prefers to take the risk and open a lingerie shop with three other people. Bautista and his partners ask for a loan of €30,000 to set up the modest business (a loan of €7500 to each of the partners is realistic). The security of receiving €430 a month and having all the hours of the day available are a good starting point for Bautista and his partners to go ahead with their business. Note that we do not necessarily assume that the four partners have low levels of risk aversion, because if this were the case their project might be considerably more ambitious than in this example. In the early days of any small business, a Basic Income might be interpreted as a subsidy that overcomes certain types of risk aversion that could appear in the setting-up phase. It would not only reduce risk aversion but would also allow greater innovation.

Part-time employment

It seems reasonable to suppose that the introduction of a Basic Income could favour the possibility of choosing certain part-time jobs that are presently not an option because they do not offer sufficient economic compensation. In the sound words of a Spanish trade union study:

> Part-time work should be a voluntary option not only to reduce the hours of the working day, but also to alternate, in the course of a lifetime, periods of working activity

with others of absence from the job market in order to engage in other activities, from training, to looking after family members and matters, or voluntary work.[8]

In the absence of a Basic Income, part-time work is subject to more conditioning factors. First, according to official statistics, many people who are now working part time do so because they do not have the option of full-time work. This is not a matter of free choice but one forced by necessity. The words of the philosopher José Ortega y Gasset (1883–1955) come to mind: 'If at any point we only had only one possibility before us, it makes no sense to call it that. It is more like pure necessity.' This 'only one possibility' is precisely what makes working part time an unfree activity. Second, part-time work is mainly done by women. In the European Union in 2000, according to *Eurostat*, 6.3 per cent of men and 33.7 per cent of women were working part time. However, there are substantial differences between countries in the north and south of Europe. In the countries of the north, part-time work is quite usual among women while, in the south part-time remunerated work for women is pretty much a peripheral activity.

Impact on levels of pay

Finally, introducing a Basic Income would have a further possible result on the labour market: a real salary rise in some jobs and activities and a possible drop in wages in other professions or occupations. If the right to a Basic Income were recognised, one might intuit that some employers offering unappealing and not very gratifying jobs would be under pressure to pay more. Conversely, as Van der Veen and Van Parijs (1986) correctly note, the average wages of attractive, intrinsically gratifying kinds of

[83]

work would tend to drop. Erik Olin Wright (1997: 22) says the same thing more forcefully and graphically:

If a worker has a guaranteed basic income it would be more expensive to bribe him or her to accept a disagreeable job. Alternatively, workers would not need so much inducement to accept interesting and stimulating jobs. There is no need to motivate sociology professors to work, for example, because their work is intrinsically agreeable.

The objection that some kinds of jobs would never be done because, with a substantial Basic Income, nobody would have a sufficiently incentive to do them has three answers. The first refers to the point I have been making about possible salary modifications, because significant wage increases in certain jobs could make them attractive (instrumentally, of course) for some individuals, if only temporarily. My second, more general response is that I don't think it would be a huge social disaster if some jobs disappeared off the map because nobody wanted to do them. Third, the fact that, for certain remunerated jobs, it might not be economically feasible to ask for higher salaries could be the occasion for technological solutions being sought in order to mechanise and automate them.

4.2.1 On the right to (remunerated) work and basic income

Now I should like to deal with one of issues that have caused hackles to rise. This is a straw man, the supposed contradiction between Basic Income and remunerated work (employment). In brief, there is no contradiction. Basic Income is in no way opposed to remunerated work.

Defending Basic Income does not mean arguing that it is

not a good thing to have a socially recognised job. Being a Basic Income supporter is perfectly compatible (and even complementary, it might be stated) with defending access to remunerated work for anyone who wishes to have it. Moreover, some Basic Income supporters have written about the advantages Basic Income might have in facilitating access to paid employment. Among these advantages[9] are the four that follow:

- A Basic Income could facilitate a certain 'spontaneous distribution' of remunerated work or employment by making it possible or desirable for many individuals to work fewer hours. Others could then cover the 'space' they leave free.
- A Basic Income might allow better access to remunerated work or employment for many individuals in different ways:
  - by doing away with the notorious 'unemployment trap'[10]
  - by permitting greater flexibility in the job market that would not translate into vulnerability and social insecurity, as is the case now, because it would reinforce the bargaining power of the weaker party in the job contract
  - by making it much more feasible for many people to accept certain kinds of jobs that they might want to do, or that are attractive but badly paid because of their low productivity.
- Noguera recalls Van Parijs' argument (1988) that the right to work could not be sustained today without the state paying massive subsidies to business and adds: 'Basic Income is precisely a strategy that attempts to provide the right to an income for everyone but not at the cost of the right to work. Rather it consists in distributing employment subsidies directly into the hands of potential employees so that they (and not the employers) can decide what jobs merit the subsidy.'[11]

[85]

- With Basic Income, the conditions for greater self-respect would increase thanks to the different kinds of work that might be done, as long as they are not 'artificial' jobs guaranteed by the state as 'assistance' to the unemployed. If to this we add the fact that (as I detailed in Chapter 3, Section 3.6.2) the bargaining power of the potential employee (the weak party in the job contract) is enhanced because of Basic Income, the salaries for disagreeable jobs should rise, or the conditions be made more acceptable, in order to generate a sufficient supply of labour. Basic Income would mean increasing the possibilities of job choice (instead of making people stagnate in the 'unemployment trap' or in absurd and demeaning guaranteed workfare jobs).[12]

Finally, it is also worth stressing the crucial point that Basic Income would not discriminate between people who have paid work and others who engage in domestic or voluntary work. Everyone would receive an income, which would then raise the degree of comparability between the three kinds of work I have mentioned.

4.3 BASIC INCOME AND DOMESTIC WORK

The second type of work in my typology, domestic work, is also called reproductive or caring work and it has many definitions. This is a symptom of the difficulties involved in trying to encompass both its activities (looking after the old or very young, cleaning, cooking …) and the different forms of family cohabitation. Nonetheless, there are some constants in all the definitions. These allude to the activities of attention and caring carried out in the home, which aim to satisfy the needs of all the members of the household from the oldest to the youngest. Taking all the constants, it is possible to produce a synthetic definition as follows: domestic labour is that carried out in the home to attend to one's own needs and those of others, and it includes activities such as cleaning, preparing meals, shopping, and looking after children and old people along with any sick members of the family or within the unit of cohabitation.

One of the earliest definitions of domestic production was offered more than 70 years ago by Margaret Reid in her pioneering work *Economics of Household Production* (1934). This definition has in turn given rise to many others. For Reid, domestic production includes non-remunerated work carried out by and for members of the family, activities that can be replaced by products on the market or remunerated services when circumstances such as income, the situation of the market and preferences make it possible to engage the services of somebody outside the family. Reid views domestic production from the standpoint of a possible substitution of domestically produced goods and services by others that are produced and offered on the market.

Going into further detail, it is interesting to note the following characteristics of domestic labour:

- It uses goods acquired on the market or through services offered by public administrations, to produce goods and services destined for home (or individual-) consumption, but not exchange.
- There is no monetary payment.
- The basic aim is reproduction of the labour force (an immediate result being reduction of subsistence costs).
- It occurs in conditions in which the person who carries out this work establishes some control over working rhythm and timetables.

Domestic work is carried out by both sexes, but by no means proportionally. In both rich and poor countries, women do by far the greater share of domestic work. Different studies (for example, Alba, 2000; Gershuny, 2000) demonstrate this tremendous imbalance between the sexes. In the European Union, more than 80 per cent of women who have children at home spend four hours every day on household tasks, while only 29 per cent of men spend this much time. In the case of Spain, for the years 2002–03, a survey of 46,774 people showed that women spent an average of four hours twenty-four minutes every day on tasks pertaining to 'home and family'.[13] Men spent one and a half hours on the same tasks, which is to say one-third of the time spent by women.

It is also interesting to note the elasticity between remunerated work and domestic work. There is no doubt that the less time that is spent on remunerated work the more is spent on domestic work, but the proportions between the sexes are very different. Women devote much more time to domestic work when they spend less time on remunerated work. Men devote only a little more time to domestic tasks in these circumstances. This is hardly new, so I shall not dwell on it any further.

What does deserve a little attention, however, is the not very consistent habit of considering the same – exactly the same – activity as work in some cases and as non-work in others (cooking, for example). The same simple fallacy appears once again in a slightly different guise: only an activity for which one receives monetary remuneration can be called work. It would surely be more consistent to think that the same activity could be included under different types of work. Imagine that I am washing a lot of patterned underpants at home. It might be remunerated work, voluntary work or domestic work, depending on whether I am charging for this, or doing it for some voluntary association in my neighbourhood or doing it for myself and my large family. I should like to underline the following point. If washing underpants is seen as work, it will be work in all three cases. If it is not seen as work then it should not be seen as work in any of the three cases. What is shocking is that it is considered as work only when monetary remuneration is received.

Although the inclusion of domestic work under the heading of work has become more widespread in academic circles in recent years, evaluating it is more problematic. This involves major problems of measurement. The methods that have been developed can be grouped into two main blocs.[14] First are those that focus on the quantity and quality of the work used to obtain goods and services, and that are therefore based on input. Second are methods that focus on the value of the product obtained, and are thus based on output. Once again, the input-based methods can be divided, depending on the mechanisms used, into a) replacement costs, b) service costs and c) opportunity costs. The output-based methods can also be divided into a) total product and b) added value. On the basis of these different approaches to quantifying domestic work, a number of empirical estimates have been made of the percentage participation of domestic work in relation to the gross domestic product (GDP) in different countries. In general, the total of all the types of work that have been used to quantify domestic work as a percentage of GDP varies between a half and two-thirds of GDP. Whatever the upper and lower limits of the figure, it cannot be denied that domestic work, leaving aside the differences of mechanisms used to measure it and the finer points of the results obtained, represents in all cases a truly significant percentage of GDP.

These percentages only have an indirect value in making us see the proportions of the kind of work that has not been counted in the traditional calculations of economists. There are some objections as to the utility of these comparisons. Some people point out that productivity in remunerated work on the market is not the same as it is in domestic tasks. It is also true, however, that not all of the activities that come under the heading of remunerated work are readily comparable either. Apart from criticisms that can be made over possible margins of errors in this data, what needs to be stressed is the importance of domestic work, which has been concealed by standard reckonings in economics. This importance not only resides in the more or less high percentage of GDP that it might represent. For example, a mother's love and devotion cannot be calculated in market terms, but the GDP factor should not be overlooked.

I have given some idea in the previous chapter (Section 3.6.1) of how Basic Income could be a good means of achieving the material existence of many women, and now I should like to look at its relationship with domestic work itself. How might domestic work be affected by the introduction of Basic Income? A general aside is relevant here before I answer this more specifically. Basic Income alone will not resolve all the social problems related with the sexual division of labour. I make the point because of the frequency with which one reads or has to listen to hot-air (and highly inconsistent) criticisms of Basic Income decrying the fact that it will not put an end to certain social problems that it simply does not aspire to resolve or even directly address. To carp about the dole because it doesn't help with housing problems or the public health system, or because it doesn't do anything about youth unemployment seems more than a little unreasonable. Yet this often happens with Basic Income. Sexual inequalities and the gender-based division of labour are two major social problems whose solution (if we think there is a clearly identifiable 'solution') lies in a packet of much more sweeping reforms than Basic Income. This noted, I shall now look at the question of how Basic Income might affect domestic work.

First, it would permit greater development 'in terms of life opportunities for women – at any stage of their life cycle'.[15] There are many women (and men of course, but fewer) who do not have much choice in this regard at present. Even minimal economic independence would considerably open out the opportunities of these women. As early as the eighteenth century, Mary Wollstonecraft (1759–1797) was saying, as Carole Pateman (2003: 140) has recently recalled, that rights, citizenship and the position of women required 'among other radical changes, economic independence for both married and single women'.

Second, many women who are caught in the poverty trap within the present-day system of means-tested subsidies (which I shall discuss further in Chapter 6) could escape from it with a Basic Income. The feminisation of poverty would be significantly mitigated. Recall that Basic Income is universal and thus paid to both men and women. It follows that, in Laura Pautassi's words (1995: 270), at least some problems 'deriving from assigning allowances to the "head" of the family on behalf of "dependents" ... where it is implicitly understood that he will be the one to decide what to do with the money' would be avoided.

Third, the introduction of a Basic Income could change the distribution of domestic tasks between men and women in households where this applies. In cases of gay couples, house-sharing friends or people who live alone (a fast-growing reality in rich societies), or in situations like nunneries and monasteries where men and women do not live together, it does not apply. The negotiating power in the home of a woman receiving a Basic Income would be greater, but whether by a lot or a little depends on the case. This said, I return to what I remarked above about not asking more from Basic Income than it can give; with regard to the distribution of domestic tasks between men and women, it could make some things easier for women but not much more.

Further social and cultural changes would be required to attain true equality of treatment and proper sharing of domestic tasks between men and women.[16]

In conclusion, and in the highly condensed synthesis of Vanderborght and Van Parijs (2005: 68), 'In relation with men, women would gain enormously with the introduction of a basic income, both in terms of income and freedom to choose'.

4.4 BASIC INCOME AND VOLUNTARY WORK

Finally, we come to the third category of voluntary work. This is understood as using one's own time in unpaid activities devoted to others without coming under the rubric of domestic work.[17] Voluntary work occurs in a wide range of areas, a few examples among many being social services, medical care, education, solidarity with the poor, work rehabilitation projects with prisoners, counselling of battered women, care of AIDS patients, solidarity work with populations affected by natural disasters and third-world solidarity work.

The motivation for engaging in voluntary work may be twofold. First is personal satisfaction in the activity itself. Strictly speaking, this would be a case of the autotelic type of activity to which I referred at the beginning of this chapter, and which I shall discuss in a little more detail now. The reward of an autotelic activity is the activity itself or, as Domènech (1989: 349) puts it: 'The process is what counts, the way itself is the goal.' Instrumental activity is the opposite of autotelic activity because the process is secondary; it is necessary for reaching a goal, and the goal is what counts. Remunerated work, with some exceptions is instrumental. Given the need to acquire a series of essential items (food, house, clothes and so on), one needs money and for most of the population remunerated work is the only way of getting it. Wage work is a very important subset of remunerated work, the only option for people who own no more than their labour power, and as I have suggested earlier, speaking of 'option' when there is no option is a curious juridical fiction. Hence, for almost all the population, wage labour is instrumental, a means, a way of satisfying certain needs unrelated to the work. However, it would be very difficult to understand voluntary work if we do not understand it as essentially autotelic[18] and non-instrumental.[19]

The second motivation of voluntary work might be benevolence or altruism, understood as genuine concern for the welfare of the person or people who benefit from the voluntary work.[20] However, whether benevolence is purely altruistic is a moot point because the psychological feel-good effect or the desire to be admired as a good person or similar motivations could be quite instrumental factors. In short, this second benevolent motivation is related to the first, even if they can be conceptually separated.

The introduction of a Basic Income could mean, for reasons that are evident enough in themselves, a stimulus for more participation in voluntary work. Given its nature, volunteering requires more time than people normally have available. One cannot view voluntary work as an 'alternative' to remunerated work precisely because, in the absence of other sources of income, the latter is essential for survival. If this constriction is at least partially eased by a Basic Income, the set of opportunities would open up. Many people who do not presently engage in voluntary work but who would like to do so would find their chances are better. Needless to say, the possible social changes this could bring about should not escape even the most limited of imaginations.

5 POVERTY

[T]o which period had originated that numerous class emphatically denominated the POOR, consisting of those personally free, but without the means of supporting themselves by their industry or capital, unaided by the gratuitous assistance of their fellow-men. Individuals in this unhappy condition are clearly in a state of slavery; those who cannot live independently of the support of others, cannot, in the affairs of life, act the part of freemen.

John Wade (1788–1875), 1833

Basic Income is a response to poverty today, but its potential does not end here. Even if it were no more than a measure against poverty, that alone would be sufficient reason for taking it very seriously. To the extent that it constitutes a form of access to income independently of whether remunerated work is carried out or not, it is especially appropriate for societies with high and persistent levels of poverty. These are not a mere few. In poor and rich countries alike, the only change we have seen over the last decades is that poverty is getting worse, with all its calamitous effects in every sphere of social existence.[1]

One of the main merits of Basic Income as an instrument for combating poverty is that it is a highly effective means of giving more freedom to a considerable part of the citizenry.

Poverty, as I have stressed earlier, is much worse than privation, material want and lack of income. It also means dependence on the arbitrariness and greed of others, the demolition of self-respect, isolation and social compartmentalisation for those condemned to it. From the democratic republican standpoint, this is especially important because the person who is poor is not (cannot be) free. He or she does not have the conditions of material existence that are required for the exercise of freedom. This idea is the backdrop to this chapter and I shall bring it to centre stage once more at the end.

5.1 A TYPOLOGY OF POVERTY

The typology of poverty constructed by Erik Olin Wright (1994) is particularly instructive. Looking at different studies on poverty, he asks, 'What are the factors or causes of poverty?' He then sets up the following classification: (1) poverty as a result of characteristics intrinsic to the individual; (2) poverty as a result of contingent individual characteristics; (3) poverty as a product of social causes; and (4) poverty as a result of properties inherent to the social system.

In the first group, people are poor because they have some kind of inborn defect, 'generally linked to genetic inferiority affecting their intelligence' (1994: 33). The contentious index known as the Intelligence Quotient tends to be used to reinforce this way of explaining poverty. It may not be an academically prestigious approach but it is certainly popular. Wright notes that, in 1980, it was estimated that rather more than 50 per cent of the US population either wholeheartedly or more or less agreed with the statement that, 'One of the main causes for poverty is that some people are simply not intelligent enough to compete in this modern world' (ibid). A decade later, in 1991,

40 per cent of a survey agreed with the assertion. True, the numbers of those who agreed had dropped but it was still a very high percentage.

The second approach leaves aside innate individual attributes and attempts to explain poverty through cultural and social processes. This is the 'culture of poverty' thesis and it appears in more or less extreme forms. The general idea, however, is that the solution to poverty lies in making people change. This view, too, has ample popular support. In 1980, an estimated 70 per cent of the population of the United States agreed with the claim that, 'One of the main reasons for poverty is that many poor people are simply too lazy to work' (ibid: 36). By 1991 the figure had dropped but was still a substantial 55 per cent.

The third approach is that poverty is a social by-product. This time, the explanation is sought in the nature of the structure of opportunities that people have to deal with. The solution, according to this view, is to foster certain employment programmes, along with education and training of disadvantaged youth to equip them so that they can participate on the job market. There are different positions on this approach. On the negative side, conservatives say that the generosity of the welfare state only encourages irresponsibility, and therefore the solution is to change the structure of incentives for poor people by suppressing benefits and welfare programmes so that then they will have to 'stand on their own two feet'.

The fourth explanation, the most informative and sophisticated, sees poverty as a problem that is inherent and even crucial to the functioning of particular social systems, and considers that in capitalist societies, poverty is essentially caused by the dynamics of class exploitation. Now that the word 'exploitation' has appeared and since, unfortunately, it is a term that is widely used, with little rigour and in the most diverse range of contexts, I shall need to give it some attention.

Wright's discussion of the term is both revealing in itself and helpful for understanding his more general analysis of poverty.

In brief, he argues that if we break down the concept of exploitation – leaving aside the moral component that arises with any exploitative social relation – its nub is to be found in a particular type of antagonistic interdependence that appears between the material interests of different actors in economic relations. 'Material interests' refers to the options people have to deal with in pursuing their economic well-being. Saying that people have a material interest in improving their economic well-being does not necessarily mean they want to increase their consumption levels to the nth degree, but rather that they want to improve the balance of their options between work, leisure and consumption. In turn, the expression 'antagonistic material interests' has a more precise meaning. Two people have antagonistic material interests when strategies for improving the well-being of one entail inherent threats to the well-being of another. The well-being of the favoured person is not just greater than that of the disadvantaged person, but it is obtained at the expense of the other.

Antagonistic material interests can appear in many contexts (between different capitalist companies competing for raw materials or a niche in the market, for example), but Wright is more specifically interested in the context of material interests between two opposed or antagonistic classes. For Wright, if exploitation is to occur, three conditions are needed:

1. The welfare of one group of people depends on the material deprivation of another.
2. The causal relationship in (1) implies the asymmetrical exclusion of the exploited group from certain productive resources (typically property rights).
3. The causal mechanism that translates the exclusion of condition (2) into the differences of well-being in (1) entails the

appropriation of the fruits of labour of the exploited group by the group that controls the relevant productive resources.

This is a compact definition. The first condition establishes the antagonism of material interests. The second condition establishes that the antagonism has its roots in how people are situated in the social organisation of production. The third condition identifies the specific mechanism through which the interdependent antagonistic material interests are generated.

In Wright's scheme, the well-being of the exploiter depends on the efforts of the exploited as well as on depriving him or her of productive resources. If only the first two conditions were fulfilled we would have 'non-exploitative economic oppression', without the mechanism of exploitation. In the first condition, there is no transfer to the oppressor of the fruits of labour of the oppressed. The oppressor's well-being simply depends on excluding the oppressed from access to certain resources but not on his or her efforts or labour power. A colonial example illustrates this point. There can be no doubt that life would have been much easier for the European settlers if the territory that subsequently became the United States and Canada had not already been inhabited by other people.[2] The Indians were not exploited but were *only* deprived of their resources and exterminated.

Genocide is always a potential strategy for non-exploitative oppressors but not for exploiters. Exploitation defines structured processes of interaction for a set of social relations that bind exploiter and exploited. In the Marxist tradition of class analysis, class divisions are defined in terms of the link between property rights and exploitation. In capitalist society, the central form of exploitation is based on property rights over the means of production. These property rights generate three classes: the capitalists (exploiters), who possess the means of production; the workers (exploited), who do not possess the means of production and sell their labour power; and the petty bourgeoisie (neither exploiters nor exploited), who possess some means of production that they employ in working for themselves without hiring themselves out to others. The exploitation that generates the capital–labour relation has been well known since Marx's times: workers have to sell their labour power to those who possess the means of production. Capitalists, through their possession of the means of production and of property rights, and the power this confers on them, are able to force the workers to produce more than is necessary for their subsistence, the 'surplus value', which the capitalists appropriate.

However, to return to exploitation, if Xavier exploits Sergi, Xavier needs Sergi because he depends on Sergi's labour power, but if Xavier oppresses Sergi, he doesn't need Sergi. To put this differently and in bald terms, oppressors would be quite happy if the oppressed disappeared so, as I have remarked, genocide is an option for oppressors but generally not for exploiters. 'The best Indian is a dead Indian' is a phrase often repeated by some oppressors of American Indians and it can apply to Indians as a whole. Conversely, if some exploiters feel moved to say, 'The best worker is a dead worker', they cannot be referring to workers as a whole because workers are necessary. They could only refer to specific workers, unruly, trouble-making, incorruptible ones, let's say.

Poverty exists, to return to the fourth point, because of the fact that there are powerful people who have an interest in its existence. As Wright points out:

> The pivotal idea is that there are powerful and privileged actors who have an active interest in maintaining poverty. It is not just that poverty is an unfortunate consequence of their pursuit of material interests; it is an essential *condition* for the *realization* of their interests.

> To put it bluntly, capitalists and other exploiting classes
> benefit from poverty.
>
> (Wright, 1994: 38; author's emphasis)

This view of poverty can allow two major alternative arguments as to how it should be eradicated: the revolutionary Marxist and the social-democratic standpoints.[3] For the former, the only way to reduce poverty is to eliminate capitalism, while for the latter, capitalism can be partly reined in and a certain redistribution of wealth is possible.

Erik Olin Wright belongs to the first, revolutionary Marxist, group and draws the following conclusions in his analysis: (1) there might be people who are poor because they have a very limited intelligence or as a result of cultural factors passed down from previous generations; (2) this is a sadly incomplete explanation; (3) there are a significant number of people with material advantages who are exploiters or oppressors (which, as I have noted, are not at all the same thing) with a great interest in maintaining poverty; (4) any solution to poverty must take power relations into account; and (5) anti-poverty programmes should not be rejected.

One can agree with all these points or only some of them. Certainly, in order to agree with the fifth conclusion, it is not necessary to accept the other four. The Basic Income proposal fits well with Wright's fifth and final conclusion because, among its other virtues, it is a proposal for fighting poverty. Let us return to poverty itself now.

5.1.1 The working poor

With the crisis (or, rather, crises) of the welfare state, the problems arising from industrial regulation (deregulation) and the dismantling of productive networks across great geographic swathes, poverty has extended to new sectors of the population ('new' in comparison with those that existed in the 30 years subsequent to the Second World War, the golden age of the welfare state in Europe). More recently, around the turn of the century, a particularly important social phenomenon has appeared in the form of the working poor. These workers, even though they have a legal work contract, remain below the poverty threshold in their geographic zones.

The working poor have been a standard part of the labour market in the United States for years but they are a relatively recent phenomenon in Europe. If the welfare state that existed in most European countries after the Second World War was once able to exclude from the ranks of the poor everyone who had a waged job, this situation has changed drastically in the last 15 years.[4] The figures are nothing short of deplorable:

> In the European Union 3.6 per cent of the population is constituted by the working poor and, what is even more significant ... 10 per cent of the European population lives in poor low-waged homes. The countries in the south of Europe, which have the highest levels of overall poverty, also show the highest levels of low-wage poverty. The worst case is that of Portugal where more than 20 per cent of the population lives in this type of home.
>
> (Medialdea and Álvarez, 2005: 59)

Translating this into absolute numbers, it means that, in the European Union as a whole, there are more than 35 million poor workers. In the heart of the zone with the best social protection in the world, 35 million is hardly a paltry number.

The causes for this increase in the numbers of poor workers in the European Union over the last decade and a half are:

1. Real salary growth that is below the increase in productivity: in 1970, the proportion of workers' wages in the total GDP of the 15 countries that would become the European Union was 75.5 per cent, while in 2002 it had dropped just over 7 per cent to 68.4 per cent.
2. Cuts in social spending.
3. The increasingly precarious labour market.

Medialdea and Álvarez (2005: 63) sum up this third causal factor in the following words:

> Job precariousness, which arose from the reforms that were carried out in European job markets in the 1980s and 1990s, along with the demolition of the bargaining power of workers' unions is at the heart of the phenomenon of low-wage poverty. Job precariousness – this being understood in terms of temporary contracts, or part-time contracts accepted as a matter of necessity, and increasing outsourcing and subcontracting in the productive process – has meant that, for a great number of working-class homes, having a job is no guarantee of being protected against poverty.

In the United States, of the 35.9 million people considered as being poor – 12.5 per cent of the total population according to government figures in 2003 when a person of 65 years or more, living alone on less than $8825 per year, or a four-member family with less than $18,810 per year were deemed to be below the poverty threshold – 7.4 million were poor workers.[5] The labour force of the United States numbered 140 million people in 2003. Among the youngest poor workers, from 16 to 19 years of age, the proportions varied from 20.7 per cent among Afro-Americans to 11.9 per cent among

Latinos and 8.1 per cent for Whites (US Bureau of Labour Statistics, 2003).

5.1.2 Poverty and the sexes

In gender terms, poverty does not affect people equally. The financial resources of a family are not necessarily shared equally among all the members. Family unity, as many studies and simple observation reveal, does not always mean harmony and solidarity. However, to extrapolate from this that only one person dominates everything would be to fall into the trap of oversimplification. Among the different people who comprise the family one needs to distinguish who earns the money, who controls it and who consumes it. It is not for nothing that the expression 'feminisation of poverty' appeared more than 30 years ago to indicate an ever-increasing number of women among the poor population. If women were poorer than they were before (which could also occur among other sectors of the population), this would mean impoverishment among women but not the feminisation of poverty, as Carrasco et al note (1997).

The most frequently mentioned factors used to explain the feminisation of poverty are (1) unfavourable conditions on the job market and (2) the changes that have been registered in family structure. I should like to look at these two factors in a little more detail.

1. The figures for working women (a category that does not include domestic or unwaged labour) are lower than for working men in all countries of the European Union, which is to say that unemployment figures for women are higher than for men. The proliferation of present-day forms of under-employment (women constitute the group

that does most part-time work) and, in particular, wage discrimination are major elements in this first explanation of the feminisation of poverty.

2. As for changes that have occurred within the family structure, the significant rise in one-parent families in recent years needs emphasising. Although the presence of single-parent families varies considerably depending on the country within the European Union, Ayala (1998) notes that in the European Union taken as a whole a woman is the main provider in about 85 per cent of these families. The figures suggest a fairly unambiguous correlation between female-headed, single-parent families and poverty.

The effects of a possible introduction of a Basic Income on this phenomenon of the feminisation of poverty would be substantial precisely because of the nature of the problem. A Basic Income would be a frontal assault on the feminisation of poverty. First, it would offer women with few financial resources greater opportunity to choose more beneficial options in their life planning, which is to say a set of consciously sought ends and meta-ends to orient their action. This is a great deal but it should be clearly understood that a Basic Income would only improve the opportunities for many women to choose a life plan, which is very different from asserting that the plan would be fulfilled. The second reason why Basic Income can mitigate the feminisation of poverty is that it would offer women an instrument that would help them to avoid precariousness in the job market because it brings more chances for resistance against accepting any kind of remunerated work, no matter what the conditions. While this argument is by no means exclusive to women, they would be the most affected in numerical terms.

5.2 MEASURING POVERTY

Who should be regarded as poor? In the now-classic works of Amartya Sen (1976, 1980, 1992), identifying the poor comes down to (1) specifying the population that is the object of the study; (2) choosing the variables that best approximate to the economic position of the individuals considered as poor; and (3) establishing the poverty line below which individuals are considered as poor.

Let us look more closely at one matter related to how to go about measuring poverty. The idea is that, in order to define and measure poverty, the line below which anyone is poor must be specified and then, once that is established, the next step is counting the number of people below it. The poverty index will be the proportion of the population situated below this threshold. Measurement of poverty can thus be seen as two different exercises: first, identification of the poor and, second, statistical aggregation with regard to the poor thus identified in order to obtain an overall poverty index.

It is difficult to get around the fact that studies of poverty are focused on the sphere of income, because the statistical information available in this respect is more substantial than information about costs. Yet there are serious defects in the income perspective. Imagine that Teia is very close to the poverty threshold, only just above it. Roger is below this threshold or line. However, Teia's health is delicate and she has to pay out a significant amount for treatment. Roger has good health. In statistical terms, Roger would be poor and Teia would not be. So can we categorically assert that Roger is poorer than Teia? Few people would. This is only one serious objection to the 'income perspective', expressed by means of hypothetical but certainly not fantasised cases. However, alternative proposals (essentially a cost-focused perspective) raise even more problems.

The most widely accepted poverty threshold is that denoting incomes below 50 per cent of the average per capita income. Hence anybody (or any family unit) that receives an income of less than 50 per cent of the per capita income received by other people in the area under consideration is considered poor. The proportion living in poverty is expressed schematically as:

$$H = (q/n) \times 100$$

where H is the percentage of families below the poverty line, q is the number of families below the poverty line or threshold and n is the total number of families in the population.[6]

The smaller the territorial unit chosen as the object of study, the more accurate the estimates of poverty threshold and average per capita income will be. The average income of a large unit such as the European Union is not a very specific indicator for identifying an informative poverty threshold. An average income in Catalonia, Alaska or Denmark would be a lot more revealing. Again, what might mean great privation in one place is not necessarily the case in another. If we establish a poverty threshold of €450 a month, to suggest just one amount, it would turn out that in some parts of the European Union it would be impossible to survive on this, while in other areas it might not. Some authors additionally distinguish thresholds of 40 per cent and 60 per cent of the average per capita income to illustrate one or another aspect of the reality they wish to highlight. Or a grouping of incomes between 25 and 50 per cent would designate a situation of moderate poverty. An even lower level, below 25 per cent, would represent severe or life-endangering poverty. Other intervals can be established.

Another interesting question that appears in studies on poverty is the amount of money deemed necessary to eliminate it in a certain geographical area. In terms of the formula I give below:

$$Q = N_p z - N_p Y_p = N_p(z - Y_p)$$

we obtain Q, the precise quantity needed to eliminate poverty. The poverty line is z, while N_p is the number of families with an income that is lower than z, and Y_p is the average income of the families considered as poor. If we bear in mind the definition of the previously presented indicators, H ($H = (q/n) \times 100$) and I ($I = 1 - (\mu_p/z)$), which are the final product (per cent) and deviation rate respectively, we obtain the following expression for Q:

$$Q = NHIz$$

where N represents the total number of families and H and I are expressed as basis points.

There can be little doubt that the introduction of a Basic Income equivalent to the amount fixed for the poverty line or above it would be a very powerful instrument in eradicating poverty. This alone is a huge virtue of Basic Income as a means of social reform.

5.3   THE POOR CANNOT BE FREE

In dealing with the point I want to cover now, I shall return briefly to what I discussed in Chapter 3. In the republican conception, a person is not free unless he or she has a guaranteed material existence. A person is not free if he or she has every day to seek the permission of another or others in order to live ('live only with their permission', in Marx's apt and very graphic words). Evidently poverty means the impossibility of consuming necessary goods, it means difficulties of integration in a community, it means greater probability of falling prey to certain types of social pathology and it also means other material and social deficiencies. Besides all this, poverty also means depending on the greed of others, it means a lack of self respect (without which, for Rawls, as we have seen in Chapter 2, nothing seems worthy of attempting, and if any projects should have some value for a person who lacks self-respect, he or she does not have the necessary willpower to make the effort to carry them out) and it means social isolation.

If we start out from the republican principle that equality and freedom are not goals to be striven for independently of each other; if we agree that the person who is in a situation of great inferiority with regard to others – as is the case of the poor – cannot be free; if we accept the premise that great social inequalities are a real impediment to the freedom of many millions of people, then it is not difficult to conclude that the poor cannot be free. Conversely, this lack of freedom suffered by the poor, this need to seek the permission of others every day in order to subsist, only exacerbates the next incremental leap in the inequality gap.

Basic Income is a proposal that seeks to eradicate poverty. However, from the republican standpoint, if this is a goal to be pursued it is precisely because eradicating poverty by guaranteeing the material existence of all citizens is a necessary condition for the exercise of freedom. Putting an end to poverty is essential for making people equal, which is to say, equal in the more precise sense of being reciprocally free, and this means nothing other than mutual recognition of the freedom that is bestowed by having the means of material existence.

If X has depend on Y for his or her daily existence, Y will not recognise any equality (of reciprocity in freedom) with regard to X because this dependence makes X subject to an alien regime, *alieni iuris* or, in other words, 'alienated'. A poor person is always *alieni iuris* because of not having the material bases of his or her existence. There are many powerful reasons for eliminating poverty but, in republican terms, the supreme point is providing the conditions for the material existence that will enable the social existence of the person who has been excluded precisely because of poverty.

6 THE WELFARE STATE AND BASIC INCOME

Social legislation is not merely to be distinguished from Socialist legislation but it is its most direct opposite and its most effective antidote.

Arthur James Balfour (1848–1930), 1895

Welfare-state capitalism also rejects the fair value of the political liberties, and while it has some concern for equality of opportunity, the policies necessary to achieve that are not followed. It permits very large inequalities in the ownership of real property (productive assets and natural resources) so that the control of the economy and much of political life rest in few hands.

John Rawls (1921–2002), 2001

The welfare state has many different aspects but in this chapter, I shall be guided by what is directly, and also perhaps tangentially, relevant to Basic Income. Some much-discussed issues will be left aside because they are of marginal or no importance at all here. For example, the classifications of different types of welfare state that have been the stuff of a plethora of books and articles in recent years are not at all pertinent.

6.1 WHAT IS THE WELFARE STATE?

So much has been said of the welfare state, so much has been written about partial aspects of it, so concerned with it have been different academics, that just about all perspective has been lost. A veritable multitude of individual features of the welfare state (subsidies aimed at combating poverty, more or less generous Social Security services, the quality of public education, inefficiency of the social welfare system, unproductiveness of the welfare state, excessive taxes, insufficiency of certain types of public spending) have generated a surfeit of studies that have shrunk the welfare state to some or other aspect, or only a small part thereof. I do not think that all these studies, or even that most of the ones I know about are particularly interesting, and they have certainly resulted in a great deal of compartmentalisation (perhaps as a reflection of the problem). Nonetheless, some knowledge can be gleaned from all the effort expended on these aspects and details so I shall be using some products of the resulting vast exercise in pigeonholing. To begin, we need to look at the welfare state in historical perspective.

Although the welfare state that is most directly of interest here dates from after the Second World War, there are relevant antecedents that run through the nineteenth century and the early twentieth century. The 'social state' of the end of the nineteenth century and the early twentieth century, which expressed the desire of legislators for public intervention in the economy, is the main forerunner of today's Welfare State, and it is not uncommon to find writers who indiscriminately use the two terms 'social' and 'welfare'.

Lorenz von Stein (1815–1890) was the pioneer of the social state, which was envisaged primarily to deflect the revolutionary strivings of the nineteenth century. For von Stein, not unlike Balfour in the quote at the start of this chapter, the idea was to provide theoretical justification for reforms through social legislation in order to stave off the revolution that was brewing among the ever-bigger and evermore redoubtable working class of Europe. What needs to be stressed is this idea of using a well-defined form of social intervention in the form of the social state in order to avoid (or at least try to avoid) revolutionary upheaval. Taking note of these anti-revolutionary beginnings of the social state and subsequently the welfare state does not necessarily imply glossing over some major achievements of this kind of state intervention in social affairs. They too need to be borne in mind so that we don't jump to simplistic conclusions.

Experiences like that of the Germany of Otto von Bismarck (1815–1898) with its impetus to Social Security, the laws it passed on health insurance (1883), industrial accidents (1884), old-age and invalid insurance (1889), and the measures introduced by the Weimar Republic from 1919 to 1933, bringing about significant changes in the 'democratic and social state', are essential for understanding the welfare state machinery that was set up after the Second World War, at least in this part of Europe.[1] Also important is the 'historic compromise' that was forged in Sweden in 1938. This expression 'historic compromise' was to array in grandiloquence a series of agreements between capital and labour, not the least of which was that reached between the unions and management to ease the way for economic growth. The Swedish experience would be very present in the development of other post-war welfare states in Europe. Deactivation of conflict over workers' demands and the achievement of full employment were two very good reasons for learning from the Swedish model.

Some people fix the birth of the welfare state, strictly speaking, as coinciding with the Beveridge Report, which was published in the United Kingdom in 1941. The Report spoke out in favour of universal Social Security cover for all citizens 'from cradle to grave', paid for by the general state budget and financed by all taxpayers. Among the Report's many recommendations were those concerned with the creation of a free and universal National Health Service.

When the Second World War was over and reconstruction was fully underway, the pillars of the welfare state were also resurrected with two priority objectives: (1) to achieve economic growth on the basis of the most scrupulous respect for the basic features of capitalism, and (2) to compensate from the public sphere for the deficiencies of the market thereby contributing the welfare that guarantees social peace and demand.

There were three basic circumstances that made the welfare state possible in Europe.[2] First, the workers renounced involvement in decision-making, leaving it to the proprietors and, in doing so, gave up the aim of workers' control that had been one of the great socialist goals prior to the Second World War. This renunciation was compensated by more or less guaranteed material well-being, job security in a very sweeping sense, collective negotiation, some rights within the companies that were recognised by legislation, and full employment of (men of) the working class.[3] More or less guaranteed material well-being was made possible by public expenditure devoted to indirect benefits such as education, Social Security and health.

Second, a great package was bundled together including, on the one hand, economies of scale, the resulting reduction in costs and increased productivity that accompanied the mass manufacture of consumer goods and, on the other, massive consumption of these goods (electrical appliances, cars and so on) by workers who saw their real wages increasing by the year. This real increase in wages was made possible by increased productivity and salary negotiations based precisely on production increases.

Third, the industrial bourgeoisie was at the core of the property-owning classes. This bourgeoisie was well established in the different nations and more or less willing to follow Keynes's advice on practising 'euthanasia of the rentier'. [4] All these factors that made the welfare state possible functioned quite well for three decades. The period has been described by more than one writer, perhaps somewhat tongue-in-cheek, as the 'glorious 30 years'.

6.2 THE CRISIS

After the mid-1970s, all this 'glory' came tumbling down and the real world smashed many illusions about the indefinite nature of so much well-being. What seemed as if it was going to last forever was now showing very big cracks. The effects of the crisis can be summed up in three main points. First, if welfare state capitalism was a 'constitutional monarchy', the offensive coming from proprietors, management and right-wing politicians has ensured that jobs nowadays are a very long way from the security of the 'glorious 30 years' and that the capitalist company has turned into something like a neo-absolutist business monarchy.

Second, today there are no Fordist domestic markets of mass consumption, where consuming meant something similar for a very broad spectrum of the population. It is common knowledge now that cheap consumer goods aimed at the lower-income sectors of the population are imported from countries where the working class is subjected to conditions that are not far removed from slavery. Then, of course, there is the exclusive market of high-priced goods for rich people.

Finally, the industrial bourgeoisie is no longer at the core of the property-owning classes after being replaced by cosmo-politan investors and financiers of global reach who are denizens of a very different world from the one where national 'social consensus' was an imperative. [5]

What arguments have been used by the right (although some of them have also leaked through to groups on the left) to convince us of the need for the counter-reform of the welfare state? There are many but the main ones would be the following:

1. The welfare state removes from the market incentives for investment and remunerated work.
2. The welfare state is inefficient and uneconomical. 'Vast' amounts are spent on the elimination of poverty but poverty is still very much with us.
3. The welfare state entails unnecessary state giantism. This, in turn, leads to a decline in individual initiative.
4. The welfare state means taxation rates that constitute an attack against freedom.
5. It is not true that the welfare state compensates for 'market deficiencies'.

6.2.1 Market deficiencies

Point (5) above is the really important one but here I shall have to digress for a moment.[6] Standard economic theory assumes that individuals are rational or, in other words, that beliefs, whatever they might be, are consistent or contradiction-free, and that preferences are transitive. This strange assumption of rationality belongs in the realm of folk psychology and, in fact, the theory of rationality used in standard economic theory is nothing more than a formalisation of folk psychology.[7]

I shall return to rationality after recalling the two central tenets of welfare theory, according to which: (1) it is only in a society with a perfectly competitive economy that a Pareto Optimum – economic efficiency – is achieved (direct theorem); and (2) economic efficiency, the Pareto Optimum, can only be attained in a society with a perfectly competitive economy (converse theorem). A Pareto optimum is that situation in which it would be impossible to improve the level of utility of one individual without harming at least one other individual. To state it more baldly, a situation is Pareto optimal if and only if nobody can improve his or her utility without diminishing someone else's.[8] These theorems, explained in a simple and simplified form, can be translated into the idea that if agents are rational (in the way I have described in the previous paragraph) and have complete freedom in a perfectly competitive market, they will achieve an efficient, Pareto optimal society wherein nobody can improve his or her position without making somebody else's position worse. In the light of this assumption, it is no idle conjecture to ask if these perfectly competitive markets really exist. In order for them to exist, one would have to assume a set of conditions that are impossible to satisfy in real-world circumstances. Some of these conditions are very well known: constant returns to scale, positional goods, symmetrical and perfect information, non-existence of involuntary unemployment, absence of public goods, absence of externalities, and others. If the conditions are not met, 'market failure' occurs, in Bator's coinage (1958), which is to say imperfections of the pricing system that impede efficient assignation of resources, thereby justifying a certain amount of state intervention.

To turn now to the imperfections that arise when the conditions for a perfectly competitive market are not met, let us first look at public goods. A public good has two properties. It is a collective consumption good and nobody can be excluded from consuming it. Being a collective consumption good means that it is to be available to consumers in equal quantities (public lighting in a particular zone provides the same amount of light for anyone who passes by when it is turned on; free-access television programmes can be viewed by anyone with a television set, which, in turn, is a private good) and no one can be excluded. It may also be useful to distinguish partially public goods that are designated as 'mixed' or 'ambiguous', the individual benefits of which may diminish when the people consuming them exceed certain quantities or numerical limits. These public goods are then subject to 'collapse' or 'rivalry'. Pure public goods, those that are not mixed or ambiguous, are rare. The features that would define the majority of (non-pure) public goods are collective consumption, impossibility of exclusion and the possibility of collapse. Along with public goods, we also have public bads. Pollution in a particular area is an oft-cited example.

Increasing returns to scale appear with the formation of oligopolies and monopolies, or when economic barriers to entry on to the market are set up, very real-world situations in both cases.

Positional goods are those whose enjoyment lies in the fact that others cannot have them. My ultimate quality-of-life dream might be to buy a house outside Barcelona and a car that would enable me to travel quickly and comfortably to my workplace in the city centre, but if a lot of other individuals want the same and we are all granted our wish, we will be wasting a lot of time in traffic jams. Moreover, the population sharing my choice will become too big and the value of inherent scarcity is lost.

Externalities are the positive or negative effects that any activity in production or consumption by people or businesses cause for other parties, and that appear when the diffusion effects are not reflected in market prices. They can be negative or positive and generated in production or consumption.

Information asymmetries among economic agents arise in the real world because not only are economic agents not omniscient but not all of them have the same information. With perfect competition, information costs are zero but when monopolies and oligopolies exist – as not even the most unabashed defender of real-world capitalism would have the gall to deny – the omniscience of agents must be assumed, though it is clearly contrary to the facts, in order for us to suppose that rationality will keep 'functioning'.

Involuntary unemployment occurs when somebody who wants to work for a wage is unable to do so. It is interesting to observe, if only in passing, how some economists get around this instance of market failure. The story goes that if somebody is looking for paid work and fails to find it, this is not because the job is not available (not because the market 'fails') but because this person does not have all the information he or she needs in order to find the employer who would offer the job and, again, the employer is also unaware of the person who is actively seeking work. The market does not fail, according to these economists but is subject to certain information limitations that impinge on its efficiency. This argument of staunch – normally neoliberal – defenders of the market may seem to be solid but it is not. We could apply the same argument to 'excessive' (in this view) welfare state intervention. If excessive state intervention results in inefficiencies, it is not due to the intervention in itself but to the fact that the public employees involved do not have perfect information about people's preferences and some people might be giving information with misleading messages. This, it is said, is therefore a problem of deficient information that undermines the efficiency of the state intervention but in no way is it a 'state failure'. Tautological arguments can do no more than beat around the bush of superfluity.

6.3 JUSTIFICATIONS OF THE WELFARE STATE AND SOME CRITICISMS

Apart from market failures, there are other economic justifications for the welfare state, among them being (1) the existence of preferential goods, (2) redistribution of income and (3) economic stability.

Preferential goods are those for which the level of demand is lower than what is considered socially desirable. Since it is thought that their consumption should be encouraged, the state subsidises them or offers them at a price that is lower than the production cost. Not everybody has the resources to pay for the education of their children. From an economic point of view, providing such goods has beneficial results, as is clear in the case of basic literacy. The welfare state also aims at some redistribution because the market, given its mechanisms, does not put an end to poverty. Eliminating poverty or combating its most extreme manifestations has been the goal that has guided the establishment of welfare programmes and the introduction of major redistributive mechanisms. Finally, the welfare state system of social protection contributes to economic stability by maintaining demand.

However, welfare state programmes also raise intractable problems that need to be taken into account. Effectively, the welfare state has been criticised not only by the neoliberal right, as I have outlined in Section 6.2, but also by its fervent supporters. Criticism from the latter group is especially interesting because it refers us to factors that are highly relevant for Basic Income.

Some of these critics refer to excessive control over the lives of people who seek welfare services from the state. One example of this is the follow-up of some programmes of job rehabilitation, which is very invasive. Other critics focus on the administrative costs of some social services. Even if the services are efficient, these costs are at best equal to the total amount of money that reaches the beneficiaries while, in less efficient cases, administrative costs can be several times the total amount received by all the people who are beneficiaries of the programme.

The poverty and unemployment traps[9] that result from the system of incentives and penalisations of means-tested subsidies, have also been singled out as serious problems because of penalisation of welfare beneficiaries should they accept remunerated work. Since the monetary quantities of means-tested subsidies cannot be allocated above a certain low level of income, there is no incentive to accept jobs that are part-time or that offer low levels of remuneration. In technical terms, the poverty and unemployment traps can be expressed by saying that the marginal tax rate that is applied is 100 per cent, meaning that one monetary unit of the subsidy is lost for each unit of salary payment that might be obtained. These two traps appear because, in order to receive benefits, monetary or any other type, the condition is that the authorities must monitor the amount of income received on the job market. They are of particular significance in any serious discussion of Basic Income.

Other critics point to problems of coverage or the fact that there are programmes that do not reach the target populations. This deficit may be due to a range of factors, for example excessive bureaucracy, or the programmes themselves may be seriously wanting, or the target group may simply lack the information that such programmes exist.

Finally, another especially important group of critics has addressed the serious issue of the social stigmatisation of beneficiaries of certain subsidies or services. To be obliged to pass a test in order to prove want or need can mean (and all too frequently it really does mean) that people are made to feel humiliated for being 'on the dole', and this can jeopardise other aspects of their social existence.

These criticisms will continue to apply, directly or indirectly, in the following discussion of (1) the so-called 'minimum income support' programmes, a measure that perfectly exemplifies the means-tested subsidies of welfare states; and (2) the advantages of Basic Income in comparison with minimum income support and other typical measures of today's welfare states.

6.4 MINIMUM INCOME SUPPORT

Minimum income support has been introduced into many European countries in order to combat poverty and 'social exclusion'.[10] Some systems are highly centralised, as in the case of (the Republic of) France, while others are more decentralised, as in (the Kingdom of) Spain. I have singled out this type of programme because it has deficiencies or limitations that are mostly found with 'focalised' (as they tend to be called in Latin America) or selective means-tested subsidies. The problems can be divided into three groups: (1) the old problems of welfare benefits to people without resources; (2) more recent problems arising from transformations related to the crisis of the welfare state, which I discussed in Section 6.2 above; and (3) problems that are more directly concerned with programmes of job rehabilitation or incentivised paid work.

In the first group there are several points to be noted. First are the budgetary limitations of minimum income support programmes. In general, these programmes cover only a tiny percentage of the poor population, as one might expect when the budgets are miniscule in comparison with the problem they are supposed to deal with.

Then there are the poverty and unemployment traps I have just mentioned. Minimum income support means financial assistance that is non-accumulative. It complements a possible income that is pegged to the ceiling fixed by the programme. This conditionality militates against people accepting possible low-paid offers of remunerated work (the few beneficiaries of these programmes tend to be unskilled workers) or even part-time work. There is no incentive to accept such jobs, because the whole remuneration that is paid to the worker is subtracted from the welfare benefits. This non-accumulability of state benefits over other sources of income also leads to small-scale tax fraud since the short-term advantages of having two incomes (welfare benefits and black-economy work) are difficult to resist. Short-term needs tend to be so pressing that serious longer-term disadvantages pale into insignificance by comparison. These include both long-term drawbacks like the fact that black-economy work can never be taken into account in future calculations of pensions rights, and not-so-long-term problems such as the impossibility of obtaining unemployment insurance.

Social stigmatisation is no less a problem with minimum income support schemes. Some of their beneficiaries feel that they are – or are labelled as – failures for the mere fact of receiving benefits from a programme for the poor, which marks them out from other people. Also, the administrative costs of minimum income support are huge, swallowing a very high proportion of the total budget because of the numbers of staff involved in selection and follow-up of beneficiaries, evaluation of results and other tasks.

Minimum income support programmes constitute, without a doubt, a glaring example of invasive control over the lives of beneficiaries by the social services. Such control is not a form of perversity particular to social workers but is inherent in the design of the programmes. A possible beneficiary must meet a whole series of conditions in order to receive the income support and to continue to receive it once it has been awarded. These conditions must be monitored, which automatically means humiliating intrusion in their lives by the very people who are officially helping them.

. The pork-barrel syndrome, which takes the form of clientelism in allocation of benefits, has also appeared. The European programmes are relatively transparent in administrative terms. However, some Latin American programmes which are quite similar in some ways – for example the *Jefes y Jefas de Hogar* (Household Heads) programme in Argentina – have repeatedly been criticised for clientelism whereby agents concede, or threaten to withhold, benefits in order to obtain the submission of beneficiaries or certain services they might be able to supply.

In the second group of problems arising from changes that have come in the wake of the crisis of the welfare state over the last 30 years, we find that, since the minimum income support system (among other social services) is separate from the taxation system, the costs of income tax frequently exceed the amount given as minimum income support (or as other types of benefit). This generates an evident lack of equity, given that tax relief or deductions also tend to favour the middle-income and high-income sectors.

Changes in family structure over recent decades are now challenging the previous assumptions of programmes designed to meet the needs of a certain kind of traditional family. Long-term unemployment, the relatively recent phenomenon in Europe of the working poor and the feminisation of poverty are realities that have appeared more recently, in the last 30 years to be precise, and have led to a very sizeable increase in the numbers of people who do not enjoy the right to the protection that is afforded to taxpayers.[11]

The third group of problems includes ones that are more directly related directly related to job rehabilitation or protected remunerated-work programmes:

> In the former case the promise of job rehabilitation is rarely fulfilled in terms of normal conditions that are comparable with those of the rest of the stable working population. The different 'rehabilitation plans' frequently turn out to be a series of activities to 'keep the poor amused' rather than a programme with real guarantees of success. In the case of state-protected employment, the

jobs offered are in many cases disagreeable or demeaning and they are for unskilled workers so that it is difficult to achieve the envisaged goals of rehabilitation, social recognition and so on: a 'charity' job is not much better than a 'charity' income'.

(Arcarons et al, 2005: 62)

6.5 BASIC INCOME IN CONTRAST WITH MEANS-TESTED SUBSIDIES

One good way of contrasting Basic Income with minimum income support (and, more generally, with all kinds of means-tested subsidies in present-day welfare states) is to review the problems of these subsidies as I have listed them above and see how Basic Income would perform in the same areas.

With regard to the financing of Basic Income, which I shall set out in some detail in Chapter 8, it is sufficient to say at this point that if the financing scheme of Basic Income is competently designed there should be none of the kinds of budgetary problems that generally appear with means-tested subsidy programmes to combat poverty.

The poverty and unemployment traps, which are among the major drawbacks generally associated with minimum income support programmes and other means-tested subsidies, can easily be avoided with a Basic Income. This is because Basic Income is defined as a 'bottom line' or 'base' that is not incompatible with other sources of income (although, as we shall see in Chapter 8, the taxes paid once this additional income is received can and must undergo modification). There is no need to 'hide' the fact of receiving a Basic Income and neither can it be withdrawn when income is received from other sources. If someone receives an income in the form of a salary, it will never be subject to a marginal tax rate of 100 per cent although it may be taxed more heavily than it was before the person received the Basic Income. Unlike means-tested subsidies, someone who is engaged in paid work will always receive more income than another who only receives the Basic Income and this is precisely because the marginal tax rate will never go as high as 100 per cent. As we have seen in Chapter 4 (Section 4.2), Basic Income can in many cases be a stimulus to engaging in remunerated work, while means-tested subsidies constitute an active disincentive to doing so.

The unemployment trap has one dimension that is rarely remarked upon. It might be summed up thus: there can be a period of irregular or no income when a new job is taken up and unemployment benefits or insurance cease. There is also the factor of fear or insecurity about the pay packet and about not being able to satisfy the demands of the new employer and thus keep the job, especially if there are no savings to fall back on. Theoretically, if one loses one's job one can always go back and ask for unemployment benefits again, but administrative delays can be a major deterrent in some cases. As Van Parijs (1996) says:

> The risk of possible delays in receiving an income mainly lies in taking up a job at a time that coincides with ceasing to receive unemployment benefits, and people who do not have sufficient reserves are then exposed to the risk of being trapped in a spiral of debt, eviction, having the gas cut off, and so on. Even if the objective probability is not very high, the prospect of having to face these problems is usually sufficient for people to fall prudently back into the unemployment trap.

Needless to say, given the nature of Basic Income, this dimension of the unemployment trap would not be an issue because, as a regular income, it allays the fear of any hitches in receiving an income and all the worries that Van Parijs mentions.

Since it is accumulable to other sources of income, Basic Income does not encourage petty tax fraud as happens with means-tested subsidies. With a Basic Income there are no small short-term benefits that would make a person want to hide the fact of engaging in some kind of remunerated work. Basic Income is compatible with the person receiving income from one, two or more sources. In addition, with a Basic Income, it would be both senseless and counterproductive to risk the long-term drawbacks of the small-scale fraud of accepting a black-economy job that can never be taken into account when calculating possible future pension rights.

Again, Basic Income has no problems with population cover since it takes in all citizens and accredited residents. The inadequate cover so frequently associated with the standard programmes of combating poverty would no longer be an issue.

The problem of stigmatisation associated with means-tested subsidies is much more than just a technical problem. This takes us back to Chapter 2 and Rawls's emphasis on the question of self-respect (and a person who is stigmatised by receiving a means-tested subsidy is usually a person with little or no self-respect) without which nothing seems worth attempting. In one fell swoop, Basic Income does away with the 'social failure' stigma that many people associate with the fact of receiving any kind of poor relief because every citizen would receive a Basic Income and therefore nobody is 'marked' by the fact of receiving it.

The administrative and management costs that are so exorbitant in the means-tested subsidy programmes in proportion with the overall amounts assigned to the target population are greatly reduced in the case of Basic Income. In proportional terms, there can be no doubt about this, because the amount received by the beneficiaries as a whole would be much greater. Besides, expenses are considerably reduced in absolute terms because, as it is not difficult to imagine, the costs of guaranteeing the payment (most probably every month) of the Basic Income without having to engage in any kind of checking up on recipients (amount of income, state of need and other investigations) do not involve very steep outlays on staff wages.

The serious problem of interference by the social services in the lives of beneficiaries, which is so characteristic of means-tested subsidies and especially minimum income support programmes, never arises with Basic Income, as is once again evident, because of the fact that it is universal. The only requirement is accredited residence but the invasion of private life (for example in investigating sources and level of income) disappears.

Basic Income is a good antidote to clientelism and administrative arbitrariness (a problem that is particularly germane for anyone who analyses social life from the democratic republican point of view, as I do). It does away with opportunities for discretionary treatment in bestowing or denying means-tested subsidies, so abuse of power by less-than-scrupulous public servants is much less likely. Since Basic Income is not tied to any conditions other than the recipient being a citizen or accredited resident there is zero room for this kind of arbitrary or corrupt treatment.

Basic Income can be financed in different ways but if the financing scheme becomes an integral part of the taxation system, that would mean greater distribution of income from rich to poor and would also improve fiscal accountability. Integrating the system of social services into the taxation system, which Basic Income permits, would favour a much more equitable system than what we have at present (as I shall demonstrate in detail in Chapter 8).

Basic Income is an individual payment, independent of cohabitation arrangements, which is to say it is not conditioned by any particular household arrangement. A group of friends may live under the same roof, or a same-sex couple or a heterosexual couple, or people of different generations, and the Basic Income is still paid to each person as an individual. This feature means that it is very well adapted from the outset to the changes in family structure we have seen in recent decades.

Likewise, Basic Income is an effective response to the failure of minimum income support (and of means-tested programmes in general) to cope with transformations in the job market in the last few years: increasing levels of long-term unemployment, the greater numbers of working poor – especially women – very precarious contracts for a high percentage of the working class, and other causes of insecurity. Many people affected by these changes are not eligible for contributory benefits. Basic Income, however, is perfectly able to address such situations and avoid discrimination.

Finally, in comparison with means-tested subsidies, Basic Income, since it is unconditional, is not affected by whether one succeeds in job rehabilitation programmes or not. This means, and it is not an insignificant virtue, that some remunerated 'charity' jobs would disappear off the map along with all the condescension that is associated with them.

6.5.1 Basic Income and the welfare state: what is the relationship?

All too frequently, uninformed or unscrupulous critics of Basic Income have crudely tried to claim that Basic Income is incompatible with the welfare state. Sometimes this takes the form of the assertion that Basic Income would be financed through cutting back the great advances made by the welfare state in some rich countries, in public health and education, for example. Indeed, it would make sense to criticise Basic Income for its supposed opposition to the welfare state if the aim were really to finance it by cut-backs in the education and health services or by dismantling them completely. Apart from this being an enormous financial blunder, no Basic Income supporter would support such a proposal. There is little doubt that if a Basic Income were financed in this way, the poorer members of the population would be even worse off than they are at present.

However, there is a valid question about the relationship between Basic Income and the Welfare State, and this is whether the extant welfare state would continue to exist if there were a Basic Income, or if this would mean its total demise. Some Basic Income supporters prefer to see it as a proposal that would reinforce the principles of the welfare state, while others, although perhaps less keen on the welfare state, still see Basic Income as being quite compatible with welfare principles. There are others, a minority group perhaps, who believe that Basic Income is something entirely different: that while there may be some similarities with some principles of the welfare state, there are also major basic differences.

There are always people who, being both admirers of the welfare state and in favour of Basic Income, will try to over-emphasise compatibilities. There are others who, as not such great admirers of the welfare state but keen supporters of Basic Income, will be quick to find clear discrepancies in the two conceptions. One can always find somebody who is more inclined to see continuity and somebody else who is more prone to detecting rupture. However, if Basic Income means decom-modification of the labour market, even if only partially, as we have seen in Chapter 3 (Section 3.6.2), if it means greater freedom to choose the balance in our lives of remunerated, domestic and voluntary work, if it can offer workers a resistance fund (Casassas and Raventós, 2007) to maintain strikes that are presently difficult to sustain because of the salary cuts they involve, if it means that a lot of women can cut loose from financial dependence on their husbands, and if, in brief, it can offer greater freedom to a considerable percentage of citizens because, for the first time in the history of our species, they would have their material existence guaranteed, I think there are sufficient reasons for maintaining that there are more elements at variance with the welfare state (which is based, *inter alia*, on the outdated 'assumptions' of full masculine employment and security in workplace and wages) than elements that represent continuity. After 30 years in which decision makers in big transnational companies have undertaken an offensive strategy – and it is a battle they have partly won – to put paid to the security and material well-being that a large part of the working population of Western Europe and the United States had achieved, and after the associated structural changes that have taken place over these 30 years, there is good reason for thinking that things will never go back to what they were before. In any case, if Basic Income could bring about the changes I have so briefly mentioned, we would be talking about a very different world from what we have at present.

7 BASIC INCOME IN COMPARISON WITH OTHER PROPOSALS

No one is more extremist than the true moderate because he is never moderate enough. There will always be somebody more moderate than the moderate, who will take him to task for not being sufficiently moderate. And one cannot be moderately moderate.

Marco D'Eramo, 2007[1]

In one sense, the need for revolution is plain realism. No enlightened, moderately intelligent observer could survey the state of the planet and conclude that it could be put to rights without a thorough-going transformation. To this extent, it is the hard-nosed pragmatists who are the dewy-eyed dreamers, not the wild-haired leftists.

Terry Eagleton, 2003

In comparing Basic Income with traditional (that is, older) and non-traditional (more recent – although it might be more precise to call them 'not-so-traditional') measures against poverty and unemployment, I make the distinction in a merely indicative sense, without pretensions to any theoretical high-flying. My aim now is to compare Basic Income with other measures that either have some similarities or have been proposed by different authors as possible 'intermediate steps' towards a Basic Income. Notable among the former group are the so-called 'flexibilisation' of the labour market and reduction of working hours. Among the latter – non-traditional – measures, active employment policies and workfare deserve special attention. Finally, I shall discuss policies that have some similarity with Basic Income, for example negative income tax, basic pension and the stakeholder grant. For all the similarities, I hope to demonstrate that Basic Income would be the most effective first step towards the 'thorough-going transformation' that is so needed to put the planet to rights.

7.1 TRADITIONAL MEASURES AGAINST POVERTY AND UNEMPLOYMENT: A MORE FLEXIBLE LABOUR MARKET AND REDUCTION OF WORKING HOURS

An explanation for the resurgence of the Basic Income proposal in the early 1980s may be sought in the growing evidence that traditional measures to combat poverty and unemployment were either not effective or were much less so than they had been. These included increasing the flexibility of the labour market and reduction of working hours.[2] The former is favoured by the right wing of the political spectrum while the latter is generally promoted by the left and trade unions. At different times both policies have made some inroads against unemployment but since, in general, they have proved to be inadequate at best, Basic Income becomes an increasingly interesting alternative.

It is no secret that being unemployed in rich societies, especially over a long period, is one of the main reasons why people become impoverished. This fact provides the justification for pushing for increased flexibility in the labour market, in particular by right-wing policy-makers and employers, as a partial remedy for unemployment. Unfortunately, like other hackneyed terms that are so repeatedly trotted out in the face of grave problems, 'flexibility of the labour market' is employed to mean very different things.[3] The concept (or similar ones such as 'liberalisation' of the labour market) encompasses several kinds of labour flexibility: (1) external quantitative, (2) internal quantitative, (3) qualitative and (4) salary.

External quantitative flexibility covers all measures that attempt to square the number of workers in a company with the volume of business. The business volume is variable and the aim is to make the number of employees depend precisely on its fluctuations, thereby making workers take the burden of market hiccups. This increase or decrease in the number of workers according to the winds of change in the volume of business can be achieved in different ways. First is the part-time contract, the argument being that some activities can be done in less than a whole working day. Second is hiring workers according to the time deemed necessary to meet the company's requirements. Third is using the excuse of economic difficulties the company might be experiencing to cut its labour costs, which generally translates into forced worker 'redundancy' and dismissals.

Internal quantitative flexibility includes the set of measures a company might adopt with the aim of keeping its staff members fully employed. There are at least three different types of flexibility that come under this rubric: geographic mobility; changes in working hours (depending on the season of the year, for example) or introduction of new shifts so as to make more intensive use of the company's resources; and functional mobility or polyvalence, which means that a worker is expected to carry out a range of tasks requiring different technical skills within the same company.

[133]

The argument for *qualitative* flexibility takes as its starting point the idea that developing new professional skills and cooperation among staff who participate in a particular process will help the company adapt to new service or production requirements. The faster the changes occurring in a company's activities, the more important it will be for the company to be able to adapt creatively to new demands.

The fourth approach to increasing the flexibility of labour relates to *salaries*. The idea is simple. Salaries have to be adapted to the changing needs of the company. There are different versions of this, one of the most important being making wages dependent on the company's turnover.

Some of these forms of labour flexibility are compatible with each other, but some are not. To give one example, the first – increasing external quantitative flexibility – is not compatible with qualitative flexibility. Developing new professional skills and cooperation among staff members in different areas of the company's work would be difficult or impossible if the company is constantly making changes in the composition of its personnel.

In the European economic space and the United States, pressure to make the labour market more flexible has become increasingly widespread over the last two decades. Unemployment, however, has not changed greatly in this period. The forecast for 2007 in the twelve European Union countries of the eurozone is 8 per cent at the lowest official estimate. This means 19 million people. Upholders of total flexibility of the labour market always come up with the same old humbug, claiming that the job market has never been totally liberalised as it should be. They allege that measures to achieve partial flexibility are a deformation of complete flexibility and, if the job market were completely flexible, unemployment figures would drop substantially. It is difficult to dredge up any serious empirical arguments in support of this. Real-life experience in the European domain does not establish any irrefutable correlation between greater flexibility and lower unemployment. This, it is true, is not yet an answer to the assertion that 'complete flexibility' would achieve this. Although, from a logical point of view, the argument might hold up in the form of 'a little of something can bring bad results while the whole of it brings good results', this still does not seem very reasonable when applied to the job market if we take the many available indicators into account.[4] Even if total flexibility led to less unemployment, there would still be one obstacle that I think is insuperable: the costs for most vulnerable members of society would be far too great. Their lives would be even more difficult than they are at present.

Increasing the flexibility of the labour market, it should not be forgotten, is also a measure that supposedly favours full employment, which, as it was conceived in Western Europe in the 30 years following the Second World War, is no longer possible. Some people might argue that it would ideally be possible, but 'ideally' can only mean that it would entail working conditions that would not be far removed from slavery.

Basic Income proposes that every citizen and accredited resident should have an income but not at the price of sacrificing the right of deciding whether or not to engage in remunerated work. With a Basic Income, people would determine for themselves the place that remunerated work would have in their lives, as an option rather than as a necessity. Introducing more flexibility into the labour market, as it functions in the real world today for the immense majority of the population whose livelihood depends on remunerated work, has nothing to offer that would make it worth considering. However, a Basic Income could permit some of the forms of flexibility I have discussed without necessarily entailing greater vulnerability and weakness of the workers' position, which is what happens under present conditions. Flexibility and job security could go hand in hand.

One of the measures against unemployment (and hence indirectly against poverty) that has given rise to most debate at different times and in different places over the last 20 or 30 years is reduction of working hours. As with any major social debate in which different interests are at stake, this one has thrown up solid arguments, mediocre reasoning and something very like pure-state demagogy. Leaving aside fantasies that go along the lines of, 'a reduction in working hours that leads to millions of hours being freed will mean as many jobs as the result of dividing those millions of hours by the hours in the legal working day,' I shall move on to consider this proposal with particular attention to its repercussions on unemployment.

The idea of reducing working hours tends to be accompanied by the more general idea of sharing out existing jobs. This is where the first difficulty appears. As I remarked in Chapter 4, there is certain confusion between wage labour or, more generally, remunerated work and work per se. When a proposal of reduced working hours is presented as a means of job sharing, it should be made clear that it refers to something that is much more specific than 'work'. It only refers to paid work or, to put it more simply, employment. The aim, then, is to distribute paid employment among those who depend on a wage in order to live.

Other analytical distinctions that need to be made can be exemplified with a question: who will finance this initiative of reduced working hours? This may be the lot of the workers who agree to a reduction in the hours of their working day, or of the company owners, or both groups, or the government, or some combination of the three. If the working day is reduced and salaries are maintained, the measure is equivalent to a rise per hour for the worker. All other factors being equal, labour costs would increase and profits would therefore fall. Even though 'other factors' do not necessarily have to remain equal, because the increased labour costs could be partially or totally offset by reducing other non-labour operational costs, the assertion still holds: an increased salary per hour, *ceteris paribus*, cuts profits.

If the workers themselves take a wage cut to finance reduced working hours, this can take at least two different forms: (1) a drop in salary that is proportionally less than the reduction in working hours, in which case, the financing of the project would be shared by workers and employers with a proportionally higher cost for the latter; (2) a drop in salary that is proportionally more than the reduction in working hours, in which case the employers would share the financing but the workers would shoulder a relatively greater cost.[5] An extreme case of (1) would be that where financing the reduction in working hours was borne exclusively by the employers, while an extreme case of (2) would be that where the workers bore the total cost (which is closer to what has been happening in some cases in the last ten years).

It would perhaps be helpful to establish some simple relationships that might save a lot of words.[6] If Y is the value of production in a particular economic space, L the number of workers, h the duration of the working day expressed in hours and, finally, q is productivity per hour, we can establish the following proportion:

$q = Y/Lh,$

from which $Y = Lhq$

The second formula should be read as follows: the value of production is equal to the sum of the number of workers multiplied by the number of hours that are worked multiplied by productivity per hour. If we now shift these formulas to growth rates and establish that *j per cent* (the percentage of the reduction in working hours) is equal to – *h per cent,* we then have,

$$L \ per \ cent = Y \ per \ cent + (j \ per \ cent - q \ per \ cent)$$

This in turn might be expressed as follows: the employment growth rate is equal to the percentage increase in production plus the result of subtracting the percentage of increased productivity per hour from the percentage reduction of the working day.

Without losing sight of our previous considerations we also need to distinguish, with regard to reduction of the working day, between two variables that, in combination, can give rise to four possible scenarios of different consequences for reducing unemployment. These are the intensity of the reduction and the period of time over which it occurs. More explicitly, the reduction in the working day can be (1) high intensity (let us say 20 per cent or more), or (2) low intensity (below 20 per cent). Again, the reduced working day can be introduced (a) progressively or (b) all at once. Any of the four possible combinations (1a, 1b, 2a and 2b) will have very different effects on unemployment. I shall focus on the measure that has produced the best results in reducing unemployment. I refer to 1a, reducing the working day by at least 20 per cent and introducing the measure all at once.

Taking all these relations and assumptions into account, a one-off reduction to 32 hours per week in the economic space of Spain would seem unlikely to reduce current unemployment figures by any more than 20 or 25 per cent. The reason is clear enough. Cutting back the working day would not have equal effects in the different sectors of economic activity, and within each of these sectors the differences between companies can be very great. Cutting back the working week to 32 hours in one move would, in the view of Albarracín and Montes (1993), have effects on employment that 'would, at the most, mean a growth of 3 or 4 per cent, or between 300,000 and 400,000 new jobs in the case of the Spanish economy'. Furthermore, these two writers state that this reduction in working hours might have a greater effect on unemployment in a better situation than the one that existed at the time they were writing 14 years ago. I shall therefore make an assumption that is difficult to verify but nonetheless useful for my line of argument. The idea is to multiply by three the number of new jobs created, in keeping with the relation I have just mentioned, on the assumption that this reduction in the working day occurs in a better economic situation than the one Albarracín and Montes were talking about. This would mean that between 900,000 and 1,200,000 new jobs are created. This is a considerable number but it would still leave about a million people unemployed.[7]

This kind of speculation, however, is pie-in-the-sky, playing at God with no grounding in real-world circumstances. Today's reality points to longer working days without proportional economic compensation for workers who are facing a threat that has become no stranger to industrial relations in recent years: closing down production in one country and setting up in another where labour costs are cheaper, a phenomenon euphemistically known as offshoring. Nonetheless, the argument above and the mathematical relationship drawn from it are useful if only to demonstrate that some commonplace ideas on the matter, for example the notion that X hours freed from the working day will mean Y jobs when Y is equal to X divided by h (duration of the working day expressed in hours), belong in the realms of Cloud-cuckoo land.[8] Furthermore, in recent years the unions have shown no interest in pushing for any swift reduction of the working day by 20 per cent or even 10 per cent, which makes this playing at God an even more unworldly activity.[9]

As I outlined in Chapter 4 (Section 4.2.1), Basic Income would achieve some of the aims of reducing the working day for waged workers. It may be a less direct approach but it would be much more effective. Basic Income is not only compatible with reducing the working day but also enables people to distribute their time between the three kinds of work (remunerated, domestic and voluntary), with no discrimination between people who are engaged in remunerated work and others doing domestic or voluntary work. Since everyone would be receiving an income, the social value of the three kinds of work would be much more balanced than at present and a reduction of working hours freely chosen by workers could become a much more viable option.

7.1.1 The second cheque variation

The second cheque option is a more or less ingenious variation on reducing the working day of waged workers. In the 1990s the idea enjoyed undeniable esteem among some circles in France but today it has almost sunk from sight.

One of the best-known proponents of the social reform of the second cheque or second wage initiative was the French economist and ecologist Guy Aznar (1980, 1994). It is based on three assumptions. First, there is not enough remunerated work for everyone. Second, the scale of unemployment is too great to be eliminated by economic growth (which in any case cannot be recommended in present-day circumstances). Third, reducing the working day also cannot adequately address the problem.

Although there are different versions of the second cheque proposal, they have common features that can easily be identified. In companies where the working day of employees is voluntarily or forcibly reduced by 50 per cent, other unemployed workers will be taken on to cover the 50 per cent of working hours that are now free. If, for example, Blues &

Brothers has 100 people working 40 hours per week and cuts the working hours to 20 hours per week, it will need to contract 100 more workers for 20-hours each. Blues & Brothers now employs 200 workers to work the same 4000 hours per week as the first 100 workers had done. Who finances this operation? If it is the company, it will have to double the total wage of all the workers. Second cheque supporters discard this option as unviable. If the workers finance the change, they will receive the same hourly wage but their total income will be halved. This would be even less desirable because their acquisitive power would be reduced by 50 per cent and, worse, they would be thrown into an extremely difficult economic position. So the question remains: who would finance this? The answer is clear enough: the state. Hence the company pays out the same amount in wages, the workers receive the same as before while working half the hours, and the difference would be made up by the government. Hence, 'second cheque'.

In André Gorz's words (1997: 90–91), 'The wage would remunerate the work supplied at the hourly rate agreed in the collective agreements; the second cheque would make up for the wage reductions that follow from the periodic reductions in the duration of the working day.' Although I cannot go into the proposals for financing the second cheque in any detail, it is not difficult to summarise the main ideas. First, because the second cheque would be paid to workers who had been unemployed for a long time, public money would be paying out on the one hand what is at least partially saved on the other. Second, the newly employed workers would be paying more in taxes than they were paying when they were unemployed, which would mean more public money. Third, consumption would be able to increase and more indirect taxes would be flowing into public coffers. In Gorz's view, 'the main source for financing the second cheque would be a selective tax on consumption in the form of increased VAT on certain products and specific extra taxes on energy and non-renewable resources' (ibid).

To give the briefest summary, the key features of the second cheque are as follows:

- A second cheque is never paid to anyone who is not a wage worker.
- It is never paid to anyone who works full time.
- It is not directly financed by the company.
- It is proportional to salary.

The great differences between second cheque and Basic Income can also be expressed schematically. First, the second cheque is only allocated to waged workers and not to everybody as Basic Income is. Neither is it given to people who are working full time, while Basic Income is paid regardless of the hours worked as well as to people who receive no wage at all. Third, the second cheque is proportional to the wage received and Basic Income is not. The second cheque favours the option of wage work, while Basic Income is impartial. Finally, the administrative costs of the second cheque (additional monitoring to prevent violation of the rules imposed by the procedures required by this measure) would be considerably higher than for Basic Income, precisely because it is a conditional measure.

7.2 NOT-SO-TRADITIONAL MEASURES AGAINST POVERTY AND UNEMPLOYMENT

There are also a number of proposals that are 'at the point of intersection between social policy and employment policy' (Ramos, 2004: 355). These might be summarised as: (1) unemployment insurance, (2) unemployment assistance, (3) active employment policies and (4) workfare measures. Since the first two of these do not have much bearing on my discussion of Basic Income, I shall limit my focus to the latter two.

Active employment policies have their origins in the northern European models of the welfare state although they were subsequently adopted in other European countries. There are many variations on this kind of employment policy. Some are more concerned with looking for remunerated work, others offer training and appropriate technical skills to groups of workers who are in danger of losing their jobs or who are already unemployed, while others focus on job creation by means of different instruments such as employer-incentive programmes to hire more workers, promotion of self-employment and offering employment in the public sphere.

Some of these active employment policies, such as those concerned with finding remunerated work and others concerned with technical training for workers who wish to complete it, should perhaps remain if a Basic Income were introduced. Employer-incentive programmes for taking on workers should disappear because they tend to benefit employers more than workers. Rather than offering stable jobs, many employers use the incentives to establish certain jobs that will be occupied by groups for which they can receive subsidies, for example through so-called training contracts.

In any case, active employment policies should not be seen as being incompatible with Basic Income. Rather, given the characteristics of both initiatives, they are complementary, with the exceptions I have just mentioned. The conclusion is so obvious that it is difficult to deny: all the possibilities offered by Basic Income relegate any policy that only promotes remunerated work to a much lower position on the scale of overall social effectiveness.

The case of the so-called 'workfare' (work for your welfare) initiative is different. This measure originated in the United States where welfare has come to be synonymous with economic assistance, with all the discrimination and condescension that involves in the Land of the Free. Workfare measures could come under the heading of active employment polices but they have a very interesting peculiarity: the person who is participating in a workfare programme is obliged to accept a commitment, which might be to engage in some activity or undertake some kind of training, in exchange for the benefits he or she receives. In other words, people who receive assistance must give something back, usually in the form of work.

I shall base myself on the detailed analysis by Standing (2002) to summarise the drawbacks of the workfare initiative.

- Workfare measures require 'reciprocity' from people who have no resources, but this so-called reciprocity is not required from people receiving other benefits.
- Workfare stigmatises the people it is supposed to help.
- It tends to expand the black economy and thus leads to more cases of petty tax fraud.
- It reduces the rights of citizenship to remunerated work alone rather than allowing people to contemplate work in its different forms.
- The jobs that are offered are for unskilled or low-skilled workers, which also aggravates inequalities between the group that is subject to workfare rules and most of the other citizens.
- The administrative costs are high, and there is also a displacement effect since these are remunerated jobs that have a competitive advantage *vis-à-vis* other competitors in their respective markets, which is not exactly on the credit side of workfare measures.

None of these criticisms of workfare apply to Basic Income, as I have already made clear in Chapter 6 (Section 6.5).

7.3 PROPOSALS THAT ARE MORE OR LESS AKIN TO BASIC INCOME

Other measures that are more or less similar to Basic Income are: (1) tax credits, (2) household payment, (3) partial basic income, (4) negative income tax, which I have already mentioned, (5) participation income and (6) stakeholder grants. I shall now take each of these in turn and see how they compare with Basic Income.

Tax credits are payments made to low-wage workers. The most usual form is a transfer that is paid with the salary. The amount paid can vary according to the salary level and the objectives that have been established. The British government gives the following definition: 'A tax credit isn't a tax – it's money that you receive regularly. And it isn't deducted from your tax bill either – in fact you can get it even if you don't pay tax.'[10] Tax credits discriminate against people who are not engaged in paid employment because of the basic design of the tax credit, which automatically excludes anyone who does not receive a wage or salary.

Basic Income, by nature, does not discriminate against people engaged in domestic or voluntary work, which is to say non-remunerated work. Moreover, today's job market does not offer opportunities a lot of people who want to work for a wage, while others who would like to leave their paid jobs, even if only provisionally, or to work fewer hours cannot afford to do so because of the reduction of income it would inevitably bring. Basic Income permits these decisions, especially among the latter group, while the tax credit system does not.

Household payment is a variation on Basic Income proper that particularly focuses on people who live alone. Given that in wealthy societies the average age of the population is increasing, there are ever-greater numbers of homes in which only one elderly person lives. Any home with only one occupant has higher per capita costs (rent, electricity, water, heating and so on) than those shared by two, three or more people. Household payment tries to take this reality into account and divides the allowance between a part paid to each individual (to this point, it is exactly the same as Basic Income) and another part for the home, so that a person living alone would receive two basic incomes.[11] It is evident that the fewer the people living under the same roof, the greater the payment received by each person.

Partial basic income, as its name suggests, would have the same features of universality, individuality and so on as Basic Income, but with the difference that it would be lower than the amount required to satisfy basic needs and, most importantly, would be lower than the poverty threshold in the zone where it is introduced. With a partial basic income, many of the virtues of Basic Income that I have been discussing hitherto would not be achieved or, to the extent that they were, the results would be much less striking. Workers' bargaining power *vis-à-vis* the employer, or the possibility of devoting more time to voluntary activities, or greater economic independence for many women who at present have none, are some of the advantages of Basic Income that would remain practically out of reach if the payment were considerably smaller. Some might argue in favour of a partial basic income as a first step towards a Basic Income proper. This may be true but it does not make the objection any less valid for the period of transition towards a more generous Basic Income. A partial basic income may well slightly improve the lot of the very poorest among the population but the main objection still holds: the virtues of a true Basic Income would appear in a much-diminished form, if at all.

Negative Income Tax (NIT), which I have already mentioned, has some similarities to Basic Income. Van Parijs summarises three main differences.[12] First, he says:

any NIT scheme would have the desired effects on poverty only if it was supplemented by a system of advance payments to keep people from starving before their tax forms are examined at the end of the fiscal year. But from what we know of social welfare programs, ignorance or confusion is bound to prevent some people from getting access to such advance payments.

(Van Parijs, 2000)

Second, he notes that:

although an NIT could be individualized, it operates most naturally and is usually proposed at the household level. As a result, even if the inter-household distribution of income were exactly the same under an NIT and the corresponding UBI [Universal Basic Income], the intra-household distribution will be far less unequal under the UBI. In particular, under present circumstances, the income that directly accrues to women will be considerably higher under the UBI than the NIT, since the latter tends to ascribe to the household's higher earner at least part of the tax credit of the low- or non-earning partner.

(ibid)

Third and finally, Basic Income would be more effective than NIT in dealing with a serious aspect of the unemployment trap, which, while it is taken very much into account by social workers, tends to be more or less overlooked by economists. I refer to the fact that, for a person who is unemployed, looking for or accepting a job is not something that simply obeys an iron rule that your income is greater when you are working for a wage. Van Parijs observes that:

What deters people from getting out to work is often the reasonable fear of uncertainty. While they try a new job, or just after they lose one, the regular flow of benefits is often interrupted. The risk of administrative time lags – especially among people who may have a limited knowledge of their entitlements and the fear of going into debt, or for people who are likely to have no savings to fall back on – may make sticking to benefits the wisest option. Unlike an NIT, a UBI provides a firm basis of income that keeps flowing whether one is in or out of work. And it is therefore far better suited to handle this aspect of the poverty trap.

(ibid)

The idea of 'participation income' was put forward a little more than ten years ago by Anthony Atkinson (1996). This is an allowance that is paid to every able-bodied person who engages in some kind of activity that is deemed to be socially useful. Some examples of these 'socially useful' activities, a notion I have already criticised in Chapter 4, are voluntary work, remunerated work, domestic work and training. Atkinson's aim, which could well be described as tactical, was to neutralise or reduce resistance to the totally unconditional nature of Basic Income in some circles. In these strategic terms, the difference of coverage between a participation income and a Basic Income would not be very great because only the percentage of the population that does not want to do anything at all would be left out. However, carrying out the unavoidable tasks of monitoring, inspecting and even selecting people who are considered eligible for a participation income would be very costly. If part of the population is to be excluded, however small it is, this would require a lot of administrative work to determine who should be the beneficiaries. The very logic of beneficiaries and non-beneficiaries in a participation income programme would also encourage petty fraud. It would not be difficult for people to pretend to be engaged in voluntary work, domestic work, training activities or other tasks that would give them the right to receive the income.

Finally, we have the stakeholder grant, which indeed has many points in common with Basic Income.[13] The idea is that every person on reaching his or her age of majority would receive from the state a one-off grant of money. This would be financed by funds obtained from a new inheritance tax. The amount to be received, according to its supporters in the United Kingdom, would be £10,000 on turning 18 (Nissan and Le Grand, 2000). In the United States, Bruce Ackerman and Ann Alstott (1999) propose $80,000 for each young person who turns 21 with a certain educational qualification and without a criminal record.[14] For those without the qualification and with a criminal record there would be some restrictions, but the rest would receive $20,000 a year for four years after turning 21. This plan would be financed through a 2 per cent welfare tax that would go into a 'participation fund'. One important point is that the amount of the grant plus interest would go back into the participation fund on the person's death.

In other variations, in some European countries – Belgium with its *prime de naissance* and the United Kingdom with its Child Trust Fund, popularly known as the 'baby bond' – a nest-egg is received by children at birth, although under certain conditions and in different forms, to be at their disposal when they are of age.

It would seem at first sight that the whole difference between Basic Income and the stakeholder grant lies in the fact that the former would be received in regular periodic (usually monthly) payments from the cradle to the grave however long the person lives, while the latter is a one-off endowment of a particular amount. However, I think that the divide is much greater than this. In fact, it would be possible to convert a stakeholder grant into Basic Income or Basic Income into a stakeholder grant (the amount of the stakeholder grant at a certain interest rate and for a certain number of years would be 'equal' to a Basic Income at so much per month, while a Basic Income systematically transferred into a savings plan at so much interest would 'equal' an amount designated for a stakeholder grant after so many years). For some years, supporters of the stakeholder grant and Basic Income have been arguing over the relative merits of the two proposals. Again, Basic Income supporters sometimes support the stakeholder grant for different and even contrasting reasons, while stakeholder grant supporters are also in favour of Basic Income for reasons that are (apparently, at least) incompatible. Then there are all the intermediate positions that usually seem to be more sensible, and the more intransigent positions that do not offer much to the debate.[15]

From the republican point of view, I believe that Basic Income has much more to offer. Given the existing socioeconomic conditions of the new century, if it is accepted that Basic Income can be an institutional mechanism and if the aim is to guarantee the material existence of all citizens (and accredited residents), the appeal of Basic Income is very great. To return to some of the issues I mentioned in Chapter 3 (material independence for women, the possibility of combining the three kinds of work, increased bargaining power for workers and the resistance fund in case of strikes, the (partial) decommodification of the labour market and others), Basic Income would be much more effective in opening up these possibilities than the stakeholder grant, which is designed more to offer people better conditions for playing a role in the market than to deal with all these other issues. In Van der Veen's words (2003: 164), the idea of the stakeholder grant is that 'this appeals to the American dream of emancipation through entrepreneurship'.

In my description of how Basic Income compares with other measures that are more or less similar, I have not covered every possibility but only those that I believe are the most relevant or interesting. In Table 7.1, overleaf, I summarise all these proposals with two criteria in mind: (1) the requirement for labour contributions as a condition of receiving benefits, however tenuous the requirement might be, and (2) conditions related to resources or, in other words, some kind of means testing of income, earnings and other financial resources. The first kind of conditionality can be very diverse, ranging from having worked for a wage in the past, working for a wage in the present or undertaking to do so in the future. There are many variations on the second as well.

7.3.1   A question of proximity

Sometimes Basic Income supporters debate what measures might or might not lead to the future introduction of a Basic Income that is worthy of the name. It is a discussion that, while sometimes overheated, does not have much substance. I shall illustrate in schematic form below the kind of arguments that arise. Let us call Basic Income *BI* when *X* is the present level of conditional subsidies at time *t, and* then let us call *Y* a measure that is introduced at a time *t+1,* which in terms of conditionality and generosity in the allowance, is 'closer' to *BI*.[16] The reasoning of some people is that if we have gone from *X* to *Y* in a time *t+1*, we are closer to achieving a *BI* in future. If only the world were made up of *X*, *Y and BI*! Then it would seem reasonable to think that in some indefinite time *t+1*, *BI* would be even more within reach.[17] But, besides *X*, *Y and BI* the world is so full of other factors that can make *Y* revert to being *X* or even worse (or, in the terms of our argument, 'further removed' from *BI*), that this kind of 'logic' is

Table 7.1 Comparison of Basic Income with other schemes

		Means tested	
		Yes	No
Conditional on labour contribution	Yes	• Unemployment benefits or other welfare grants • Minimum income support • Active employment policies • Tax credits and other tax benefits for low-income workers • Workfare	• Contributory pensions • Contributory unemployment benefits • Universal tax credit for workers • Reduction of the working day for waged workers • Second cheque • Participation income
	No	• Non-contributory pensions • Negative income tax • Minimum guaranteed income • Tax deductions or relief	• Basic Income • Stakeholder grant*

* With some exceptions

Source: based on Arcarons et al, 2005: 74.

flimsy to the point of being non-existent. In the real world there are so many examples of what I have just mentioned that it is almost embarrassing to single out any one of them.

If we take the case of the welfare state that appeared after the Second World War, we see a general improvement between the late 1940s and early 1970s with regard to job security for waged workers, fairly homogenous working conditions, union representation (in countries without dictatorships, of course), social welfare and the like. This was a sustained improvement that might have made one think that the subsequent decades would see the same kind of progress. From the mid-1970s onwards (for reasons I have partly discussed in Chapter 6), these hopes were dashed. Let us say that the confusion lies, to put it briefly, in confusing the static approximation of a measure to Basic Income (divorced from reality) with a dynamic approximation (bearing the reality in mind).

These 'debates' offer very little general clarification while unnecessarily generating a lot of hot air. Some distinctions are needed in order to avoid this perverse and silly kind of discussion.

Basic Income should not be confused with other kinds of measures. These may be very advisable and they may have undeniable virtues for certain ends, or even in themselves, and they might be considered in relation to (1) the situation that gives rise to them or (2) Basic Income. In the former case, there is no doubt that the measures might be better, worse or almost indistinguishable from others that exist in the starting-point situation. In the latter case they will simply look more or less like a Basic Income (as I have said, a participation income is much more like a Basic Income than minimum income support is, for example).

However, it is quite another matter to say in regard to distinction (2) that if the hypothetical measures are 'closer' to Basic Income this means we are closer to achieving a Basic

Income that is worthy of the name. Maybe we are, and maybe not. Whether it is or not will depend on a multitude of other factors, which need to be evaluated in microscopic detail. Confusing the two ideas (the similarity of a measure to Basic Income being taken to mean that a Basic Income will therefore soon come into effect) can be the cause of serious errors of evaluation, which, while common, are not difficult to avoid.

There is another aspect to the same problem.[18] In evaluating at any point whether we are 'closer to' or 'further from' a Basic Income, people sometimes commit what I call the 'naïve-technical' and 'crude-political' errors. The first of these might be expressed as: 'Since there are good ethical and technical reasons in favour of Basic Income, the political parties will end up implementing it.' With this view, there is no need to distinguish between political parties, no social classes or combat between them, no groups in direct confrontation and, as a result, hardly any social conflict. There are only more or less well-justified reasons. The necessary condition of 'good reasons' becomes not only necessary but sufficient in this kind of fallacy, which I call, without malice, the 'naïve-technical' error.[19]

On the other hand, it is not uncommon to find among critics of Basic Income, the argument that I call, again without any malice, 'crude-political'. In this case, the story goes more or less, 'Basic Income is a measure that is not intrinsically anti-capitalist and therefore it is not worth wasting time and effort on it, because if we are going to put time and effort into anything we should go for revolution and not get sidetracked from the big issues.' What the 'big issues' are is not very clear at times, or not even minimally clear, but that is not a big issue here. The observation also has a converse form, by which I mean that, while there are proponents of the 'crude-political' position among opponents of Basic Income, we also find them among its supporters. Their view might be, 'Basic Income is intrinsically an anti-capitalist measure and any understanding of it that departs from this assumption or that presents it in any other way is contaminated by galloping reformism and detracts from the purity of the proposal.'

Avoiding such errors is a task that can prevent the perpetration of other fallacies that have more serious consequences. It is not difficult to achieve with just a few judicious doses of common sense and political realism, well seasoned with intellectual decency. Nothing superhuman.

8 FINANCING

> Money is like muck, not good except it be spread.
>   Francis Bacon (1561–1626), 1601[1]

Financing is one of the areas of Basic Income research where most progress has been made in the last ten or twelve years, and interesting work has been done in this respect with different geographic zones in mind, showing how Basic Income can be paid by several kinds of public institutions. Proposals have included sub-state regions, as in the case of Alaska, and supra-state political spheres like the European Union and the countries of the North American Free Trade Agreement (NAFTA).[2] The late Dutch artist Pieter Kooistra even created a foundation to promote a global basic income to be funded by the United Nations (*UNO basisinkomen voor alle mensen*).

The ways suggested for financing these different proposals have also been diverse. To give one example, in their proposal for the European Union as a whole, Genet and Van Parijs (1992) suggest that the Basic Income could be funded through a European-wide tax on pollution from use of energy after evaluating what the costs of using this energy would be in environmental terms. In a subsequent work, Vanderborght and Van Parijs (2005: 104) state that this proposal of selling contamination permits would at present make it possible to finance a Basic Income of €1500 per year.

Among the various forms of financing Basic Income that have been proposed over the last 10 or 15 years, there is one with which I am particularly well acquainted since I was a member of a Barcelona-based team that produced a detailed report that was published in 2005.[3] The proposal involves in-depth reform of the present-day Spanish IRPF (personal income tax) system.[4] We based our research on this means of financing Basic Income not only because it was possible to obtain indi-vidualised IRPF data for Catalonia, but also because a study of this tax is especially helpful in showing the resulting redistrib-ution of income and other changes that would occur if a Basic Income was introduced. The research is based on a micro-simu-lation programme that was specifically designed for the study and applied to a database compiled from a sample of 110,474 tax declarations in Catalonia in order to evaluate different policy options for tax–benefit integration, which would include a Basic Income. The study demonstrates that the proposal is viable in economic terms and that the impact of the distribution of income would be highly progressive.

8.1   AIMS AND SCOPE OF THE MODEL

Among the studies of financing Basic Income, the most interest-ing and informative are those that use micro-simulation to estimate the costs and distributive impact of its introduction. Micro-simulation programmes that work with data of income distribution and with samples of data about direct taxpayers are particularly well suited for evaluating the distributive effects of a Basic Income because the general idea behind the reform is tax–benefit integra-tion. There are programmes adapted to different geographic zones to simulate Basic Income proposals.[5] The micro-simulation model permits many variations but is based on the following criteria:

- Tax–benefit integration.
- A full, universal Basic Income to be paid directly and unconditionally to each individual, in accordance with the definition given in Chapter 1.
- This Basic Income proposal would replace any existing public cash benefit of a lesser amount. If it is higher, the Basic Income is topped up until it is equal to this benefit (in both Catalan and Spanish cases, this would occur in particular with a certain number of earnings-related state pensions or unemployment benefits, whose amounts are tied to previously existing salaries).
- The amount of a Basic Income envisaged for adults (for minors it is less) varies according to the examples chosen. In my opinion, the first of the three examples I shall discuss in this chapter is the most interesting. In this case, the Basic Income would be equivalent to the Spanish *Salario Mínimo Interprofesional* (SMI), or Minimum Wage of 2003 (which is when the research began) in twelve annual payments of €451 per month, or €5414 per year. Here we might recall that the minimum wage in Spain is low (close to the poverty line for an individual living alone, in particular in some of Spain's Autonomous Communities). However, since 2003, the present socialist government has increased the minimum wage, so that by 2006 it was €18 per day, €540.9 per month and €7572 per year.
- Minors, as I have noted, do not necessarily receive the same amount as adults. In our simulation models they are allocated 100 per cent, 50 per cent and 30 per cent of the amount determined for adults.
- The tax rates are equalised for every income regardless of its source, so that the same rate applies for both the general tax base and the particular tax base.
- Any other tax relief, allowance or exemption of the present personal income tax is dropped.

- Basic Income is not taxed, but any other additional income is taxed from the first euro.

In keeping with these criteria and, as one might expect from a politically interesting project, the aim of introducing a Basic Income for all citizens is to achieve a substantial reduction in inequality of income distribution, and greater simplicity and coherence in the taxation and social benefits systems.

8.2   DATA AND SAMPLE

The database used in the study consists of an individualised, duly stratified and, naturally, anonymous sample of income tax (IRPF) payers for Catalonia in the year 2003. It consists of 110,474 cases and is clearly representative of the main variables required for analysis of the social and family circumstances of the taxpayers: age, marital status, number of people in the household, etcetera. This large sample was used as the basis for the micro-simulation model that was developed in order to present a proposal for financing a Basic Income in Catalonia in the conditions of 2003 and to analyse its distributive impact.

Although this database performs very well for several micro-simulation purposes, it does have two major limitations when used for simulating Basic Income schemes. The first is that the sample only covers the taxpayers among the population and their households, some 74 per cent of the total. The micro-simulations do not include, therefore, people who do not pay tax, a particularly significant part of the population where Basic Income is concerned because they tend to be the worst-off in terms of income distribution. This limitation may be addressed in two different ways.

First, from the standpoint of the cost of a Basic Income, it is possible to calculate the amount required to pay a Basic Income to the population not covered by the sample, adding it to the total cost of the reform simulated with the sample. Depending on the amount envisaged for the Basic Income, there will be a greater or lesser difference between the cost of the Basic Income and the savings it would permit in replacing other benefits. Table 8.1 shows the savings in social expenditure estimated for Simulation 1, which is for an annual Basic Income of €5414 for adults and €2707 for minors. Table 8.2 demonstrates the cost of a Basic Income for that part of the population that does not pay personal

Table 8.1 Estimated saving in social spending with the introduction of a Basic Income (Catalonia, 2003)

Basic Income = €5414/year (€451/month – Simulation 1)

Source	Saving (€ million)
Contributory pensions lower than €390	1,407.1
Contributory pensions higher than €390	5,390.6
Civil servants' pensions	255.1
Non-contributory pensions	238.3
Non-contributory unemployment benefits	228.0
Contributory unemployment benefits exceeding BI	715.8
Minimum insertion income	54.2
Child benefits	450.3
Educational grants	18.8
Social security bonuses	488.2
Active income for job insertion*	2.7
Total	**9,249.1**

* Professional training, job creation grants, measures for the handicapped etc.

income tax and is thus excluded from our sample of taxpayers in the first simulation. The difference between the savings represented in Table 8.1 and expenditure on Basic Income for the non-tax-paying segment of the population in Table 8.2 is €492.7 million. This difference is therefore the deficit that Simulation 1 can accept (see Table 8.4). In the case of Simulation 2, where the Basic Income is exactly half that of Simulation 1, the deficit the simulation can accept is €1931.1 million, or the difference between what is saved in other benefits by introducing a Basic Income and the outlay on a Basic Income for the population not included in the sample of taxpayers. Finally, with Simulation 3, the deficit that can be accepted is €886 million.

Second, with regard to the distributive impact of the reform, it is true that the database does not permit us at this stage of our research to integrate the income distribution data from the sample of taxpayers with that of the rest of the population that is not covered in the IRPF 'sweep'. However, it would seem very reasonable to assume that the segment of population excluded from the sample does not pay income tax because it has a much lower average income than that included in the sample – tax dodgers and

Table 8.2 Estimated cost of Basic Income for the population not covered in the sample (Catalonia, 2003)

Basic Income = €5414/year (€451/month – Simulation 1)

Population	Not covered by sample	Cost of the BI for pop'n not covered by the sample (€ million)
Under 18	159,492	431.8
18 years and over	1,551,043	8,324.6
Total	**1,696,990**	**8,756.4**

a few other exceptional cases aside. This is an interesting point because it means that our micro-simulation model will tend to underestimate the progressiveness of the redistributive impact of the reform on the total population inasmuch as it only takes account of the sample of taxpayers. In other words, if the model (and we shall see that this is indeed the case) predicts much more egalitarian income distributions after the reform, then we can readily assume that the real resulting distribution would be still more progressive when it includes the poorer population not covered by the sample.

The second major drawback of our database is that the sample unit is the taxpayer, not the household, and there is no direct variable available that would enable us to know the number of taxpayers per household in those cases where the tax declaration is individual. Nonetheless, we have been able to estimate the number of households 'present' (1,853,232) in the population by means of an indirect method that combines variables such as 'type of income tax declaration' (individual or joint), 'number of dependent children' and 'marital status'.

An outline of some of the main magnitudes of the sample may be found in Table 8.3.

Table 8.3 Main magnitudes of the sample

Data for 2003	
Sample (number of taxpayer declarations)	110,474
Income-tax filers	2,964,232
Spouses	650,872
Over 18 years of age	3,891,310
Under 18 years of age	940,494
Total population	4,831,804

8.3 THE MICRO-SIMULATION MODEL

In this section I should like to discuss some of the more relevant details of the micro-simulation model. These are necessary for understanding Tables 8.4, 8.5 and 8.6, and the graph. I should again stress that this model of micro-simulation is readily applicable to other countries, geographic zones and autonomous communities (as in the case of Spain) by a simple substitution of an appropriate database that reflects the fiscal reality of the zone under study.

The key concepts in designing the simulations and analysing their distributive effects are the following:

- *NI* is the total sum of net incomes (including the general tax base of the Spanish income tax, IRPF), to which are added variations on the tax base (equivalent to the special tax base). This sum may be understood as a measure of the wealth of the individuals concerned.
- *BI* is the Basic Income paid out. The micro-simulation model makes it possible to introduce different kinds of payment. It may be a Basic Income that is paid exclusively to adults, or one for adults combined with one that is the same (or 50 per cent, or 33 per cent) for minors and, finally, it could take the form of a household payment. The micro-simulation model makes it possible to calculate the financing of a Basic Income of any amount.
- *QBI* is the quota paid from income tax revenue if the Basic Income is introduced. This sum may be obtained from two different assumptions that the model permits. First, one can distinguish between the general tax base (income coming from work) and the special tax base (income from any other source) and then apply to each a different tax rate according to income brackets (as with the existing taxation system), and the

sum of the two quotas will give the QBI. Second, the same tax rates and income brackets can be applied to the sum of the two tax bases in order to obtain the QBI. In either case, it should be noted that all tax exemptions and allowances for any reason (home, donations, economic activity and any others) are dropped, along with all reductions (personal and family minimums, pension plans and so on) in order to determine the general and special tax bases.

- *QTR* is the quota of personal income tax revenue under the fiscal regulation for 2003. This sum is logically constant in all simulations and it enables us to define the concepts of deficit, surplus, gain and loss with regard to the proposed reform.

- The concepts of '*gain*' and '*loss*' result from comparing the situations of before and after the Basic Income reform. Formally speaking, they are equal to QTR – QBI + BI. A positive value represents a gain and a negative value a loss with regard to the present situation. The concepts of 'winner' and loser' are derived directly from this value and the respective percentages calculated.

- Financial *surplus* or *deficit* compares the overall sum of the Basic Income with that of QBI. It should be mentioned that the resulting amount takes QTR into account.

- '*Population*' is the number of taxpayers and their dependents. This is an important concept because it makes it possible to relate the sample unit – the individual taxpayer – to the Basic Income that is paid to every household or family. It makes a great deal of sense to take this into account when analysing the distribution by deciles, which the microsimulation model permits us to observe.

- *QBI/NI, QTR/NI* and *(QBI – BI)/NI* are three different tax rates. The first two represent the tax burden imposed by the Basic Income reform and by the 2003 income tax regulations respectively. The third tax rate is essential for our purposes since it refers to the 'real' tax burden that is imposed when the 'nominal' tax rate is compensated for, assuming a Basic Income is introduced, by the amount paid as Basic Income. This tax rate is therefore what is being paid when we consider the overall effect of the reform in relation with the present situation (and, evidently, this tax rate can be negative if the Basic Income is greater than the total of the quota). These rates are also very interesting when analysing the distribution by deciles after the reform.

The results obtained from the micro-simulation model may be classified into five main sections.

First, we have those pertaining to the total amounts of the magnitudes defined as NI, Basic Income, QBI and QTR. The model also provides some useful statistics such as the mean figure, standard error and confidence intervals for all these variables. This set provides two basic results: the financial deficit or surplus generated by the Basic Income reform and the overall percentages of winners and losers under the reform.

Second, we have the distribution by deciles of all the above magnitudes, to which the model adds the concepts of 'population' and the tax rates QBI/NI, QTR/NI and (QBI – BI)/NI. This valuable information enables us to analyse how the introduction of a Basic Income affects individuals differently depending on their income.

Third, different indices are calculated with regard to inequality (Gini), concentration and progressivity (Kakwani and Suits), and redistribution (Redistribution Effect – Reynolds–Smolensky) for the variables BI, QBI and QTR. In this case, the reference variables for calculating these indices are NI and two new magnitudes that reflect the situations before (NI – QTR) and after (NI – QBI + BI) the introduction of a Basic Income. These indices are those that are most frequently used in redistribution and inequality studies in order to analyse the overall effects of any particular reform.

Fourth, information is obtained about distribution by deciles of winners and losers, according to each Basic Income figure contemplated (see Tables 8.5 and 8.6). This gives the percentage of winners and losers per decile, the global gain or loss, and the per capita gain or loss. It is a very helpful instrument in showing the distributive impact of the corresponding reform in each income group.

Fifth and finally, all these results are complemented with graphs that show concentration curves, effective tax rates curves and the distribution of winners and losers in each decile.

There are two additional possibilities offered by this micro-simulation model: a comparison between different reforms or simulations, and the simulation for typical individuals or typical households. The first of these options makes it possible to obtain the distribution by deciles for the variables NI, BI, QBI and QTR, and of winners and losers, while comparing two different simulations. The difference, therefore, consists in the fact that, in this case, the reference values are those of the first simulation and not those of the income tax structure for 2003. With the second option, one may evaluate the impact of the Basic Income reform on one specific type of individual or household.[6]

8.4 AN AMBITIOUS EXAMPLE

Of the many possibilities offered by simulation, I shall offer the three that I think are interesting for different reasons. In the first example, which is certainly the most ambitious, the idea is to find out which flat tax rate would neutrally (which is to say collecting the same amount of taxes as at present plus what is necessary to fund a Basic Income) finance a Basic Income of €5414 per year or €451 per month, and half of this for minors.[7] The simulation shows that the required nominal (but not effective, as Table 8.5 shows) tax rate would be 49.9 per cent.

We can make some remarks about the results of this simulation bearing in mind four commonsense criteria for their evaluation if the aim is to achieve feasible and desirable Basic Income schemes:

- The reform should be self-financing (meaning that there is no net deficit, so that the present amount of tax collected is maintained and the reform is neutral in this regard).
- The redistributive impact should be progressive.
- More than 50 per cent of the population covered by the simulation end up gaining (bearing in mind, too, that almost all of the population not covered by the simulation would in all likelihood gain, for the reasons outlined above).
- The real or effective tax rates after the reform (once we have taken into account not only the new nominal tax rates but also the effect of the Basic Income) must not be excessively high.

With these criteria in mind, the proposed simulation requires a flat tax rate of 49.9 per cent. For obvious reasons, a nominal tax rate can be very different from the real tax rate. This has been detailed by deciles in Table 8.5. This rate would raise enough tax revenue (€32,619.8 million) to finance a Basic Income for the individuals covered in the sample (€23,613.5 million) plus the quota of tax revenue raised by present income tax rates (€9501.1 million).[8] The reform would have a very progressive impact on income distribution as the different indices show (the Gini index, for example, would be much lower, dropping from 0.409 to 0.38 in this simulation). The figure for net winners after this reform would be 63.3 per cent (among which are included the dependent members of the taxpayer's household).

To these we would have to add the proportion of the non-tax-paying population, which amounts to the very high figure of 26 per cent. It is no exaggeration, then, to say that the proportion of the population that benefits from the reform would be 80 per cent or over.

Surprisingly, the real tax rates – (QBI –BI)/NI – would be very high only for the top part of the decile of the population with the highest income, which is to say for the rich among the rich. A telling sideline of our study is that it led to well-grounded suspicions about huge tax fraud being committed by this part of the population. If the fraud were less spectacular, there can be no doubt that financing a Basic Income would be even easier than our study suggests. In any case, leaving aside the question of fraud, I wish to emphasise here that the study is based only and exclusively on available official data. As for the rest of the population, the first six deciles representing the sector with the lowest income would have lower real tax rates than under the present income tax regime, the seventh decile would remain approximately the same, and the eighth and ninth would face a substantial but not huge rise. The real rate would go up to over 23.5 per cent only for the highest income decile (which is, in turn, broken down in Tables 8.5 and 8.6, specifying the richest 5 per cent and 2 per cent among the highest tax declarations). The main point is that the real tax rates for the first five deciles would be clearly negative.

It is important to remember that, with changes to the database, this micro-simulation study is applicable to all countries with similar taxation systems. However, it is not exportable to countries with modest public coffers, for example those of Latin America or Africa. This is not just because of the scarcity of resources but also because of problems of capacity and efficiency in tax collection. This is why in Argentina, for example, Basic Income supporters propose a programme beginning with minors.[9]

8.5 TWO MORE MODEST EXAMPLES

The second example considers financing a Basic Income that is only half of the aforementioned figure: €2707 for adults and €1353.5 for minors. In this case, the flat tax rate required would be 29.67 per cent. The surplus in finance would be €1912.4 million, which is the amount (deficit in this case) that may be accepted as the figure that results from the difference between savings on other benefits and outlay for the non-taxpaying population not shown in the sample. The interesting thing about this Basic Income is that, while it is a modest amount, it involves a tax rate that is much smaller than in the previous example. With this reform, the percentage of net gainers would be 70.72 per cent. The Gini Index would go from 0.409 to 0.404 with this second simulation.

The third example is very interesting too: €2132 per adult and €1066 for minors could be financed by the tax rates in force for 2003 when the study began (15 per cent for incomes of up to €4000, 24 per cent for incomes of €4000–13,800, 28 per cent for €13,800–25,800, 37 per cent for €25,800–45,000 and 45 per cent for over €45,000). The resulting deficit would be €882.8 million (again, the difference between what is saved on other benefits and what is paid out to the population not covered in the sample). This time, the Gini Index is reduced by a little less than in the second simulation and considerably less than in the first. In the third example and with the reforms listed in Section 8.1, a small, but not inconsequential Basic Income could be financed with the tax rates that were in force for 2003. This is a moderate example, the one that least rocks the boat, but it is noteworthy in that it demonstrates that, without touching many present-day conditions, a Basic Income of €2132 per adult and half of this for minors can easily be financed.

A summary of the data to which I refer may be found in Tables 8.4, 8.5 and 8.6, and Figure 8.1, which follow.

Evidently the micro-simulations cannot evaluate the political difficulties that go hand-in-hand with a measure like Basic Income. The political resistance of social sectors that feel they have been badly done by, and not only from the monetary point of view, is an issue that belongs to the sort of considerations I discussed in Chapter 7 (Section 7.3.1). However, I believe that these three examples, and many others that can be obtained with the micro-simulation model I have discussed, are important for what they illustrate. They may 'only' show the percentages of different groups of people who gain or lose in monetary terms with respect to the present, but this is a great deal.

Table 8.4 Main results of the three examples

	BI adult (€ p.a.)	BI < 18 years (€ p.a.)	Tax rate	% who gain[1]	Financing deficit	BI index[2]	BI index[3]	BI index[4]	Gini[6]
Example 1	5,414	2,707	49.90%	63.30%	494.70	−0.36	−0.37	−0.20	0.3803
Example 2	2,707	1,354	29.67%	70.72%	1912.40	−0.36	−0.37	−0.08	0.4043
Example 3	2,132	1,066	(5)	75.10%	882.85	−0.36	−0.37	−0.06	0.4066

1. Includes household members dependent on person who files tax declaration.
2. Kakwani Progressivity Index (for present tax quota it is 0.28).
3. Suits Progressivity Index (for present tax quota it is 0.33).
4. Reynolds-Smolensky Redistribution Index (for present tax quota it is 0.05).
5. Tax rates of different income brackets according to general taxation bases for 2003.
6. The Gini coefficient is 0.4096 for present tax quota.

When interpreting indices it should be borne in mind that they take positive values for taxes and negative values for transfers.

Table 8.5 Tax rates on net income by deciles

Present tax	10%	20%	30%	40%	50%
QTR	0.06%	0.31%	0.92%	2.03%	3.21%
Example 1	10%	20%	30%	40%	50%
QBI	49.900%	49.900%	49.900%	49.900%	49.900%
QBI–BI	−106.9%	−35.3%	−19.1%	−9.4%	−4.0%
Example 2	10%	20%	30%	40%	50%
QBI	29.67%	29.67%	29.67%	29.67%	29.67%
QBI–BI	−48.7%	−12.9%	−4.8%	0.0%	2.7%
Example 3	10%	20%	30%	40%	50%
QBI	17.199%	19.627%	20.658%	21.255%	22.051%
QBI–BI	−44.5%	−13.9%	−6.5%	−2.1%	0.8%

Table 8.5 continued

60%	70%	80%	90%	95%	98%	100%
4.63%	7.06%	10.63%	15.85%	13.66%	14.01%	27.64%

60%	70%	80%	90%	95%	98%	100%
49.90%	49.90%	49.90%	49.90%	49.90%	49.90%	49.90%
3.7%	10.9%	17.0%	23.5%	30.0%	35.7%	43.9%

60%	70%	80%	90%	95%	98%	100%
29.67%	29.67%	29.67%	29.67%	29.67%	29.67%	29.67%
6.6%	10.2%	13.2%	16.5%	19.7%	22.6%	26.7%

60%	70%	80%	90%	95%	98%	100%
22.912%	23.702%	24.648%	27.031%	29.992%	34.182%	40.516%
4.7%	8.3%	11.7%	16.6%	22.2%	28.6%	38.1%

Table 8.6 Distribution of winners and losers by deciles of net income

Example 1	10%	20%	30%	40%	50%
Winners	100.00%	100.00%	91.92%	63.69%	51.12%
Total gain (mill €)	1,358.95	889.98	702.11	615.20	620.45
Per capita gain (€)	4,584	3,002	2,577	3,259	4,095
Losers	0.00%	0.00%	8.09%	36.40%	48.84%
Total loss (mill €)	0.00	0.00	5.67	57.93	133.69
Per capita loss (€)	0	0	237	537	924

Example 2	10%	20%	30%	40%	50%
Winners	100.00%	95.92%	65.66%	58.29%	56.88%
Total gain (mill €)	622.35	345.10	273.38	258.77	268.69
Per capita gain (€)	2,099	1,214	1,405	1,498	1,594
Losers	0.00%	4.08%	34.35%	41.80%	43.08%
Total loss (mill €)	0.00	0.80	32.28	66.59	87.14
Per capita loss (€)	0	66	317	538	682

Example 3	10%	20%	30%	40%	50%
Winners	100.00%	100.00%	88.69%	81.64%	78.60%
Total gain (mill €)	569.42	368.61	300.06	293.93	300.81
Per capita gain (€)	1,921	1,244	1,141	1,215	1,291
Losers	0.00%	0.00%	11.31%	18.44%	21.35%
Total loss (mill €)	0.00	0.00	5.12	19.67	33.19
Per capita loss (€)	0	0	153	360	524

Table 8.6 continued

60%	70%	80%	90%	95%	98%	100%
42.09%	35.83%	28.87%	19.63%	12.28%	5.72%	1.84%
499.49	397.15	304.32	176.64	52.85	12.28	2.60
4,003	3,739	3,556	3,035	2,903	2,414	2,394
57.88%	64.20%	71.08%	80.37%	87.72%	94.26%	98.16%
256.42	411.28	588.12	929.14	728.42	687.07	1,339.57
1,495	2,161	2,791	3,900	5,603	8,196	23,019
60%	70%	80%	90%	95%	98%	100%
43.84%	39.38%	40.62%	36.67%	53.07%	68.52%	74.22%
218.33	189.72	179.83	155.56	115.98	151.37	499.11
1,680	1,625	1,494	1,431	1,475	2,484	11,343
56.13%	60.66%	59.33%	63.34%	46.93%	31.47%	25.77%
127.59	158.26	175.51	232.87	115.43	88.36	280.96
767	880	998	1,240	1,659	3,158	18,389
60%	70%	80%	90%	95%	98%	100%
70.21%	64.47%	62.92%	39.06%	24.99%	8.55%	5.32%
242.21	214.17	203.48	114.90	36.36	6.09	2.55
1,164	1,121	1,091	992	982	801	811
29.76%	35.57%	37.02%	60.94%	75.01%	91.43%	94.68%
53.11	67.91	82.85	208.27	196.08	281.19	822.37
602	644	755	1,153	1,764	3,458	14,651

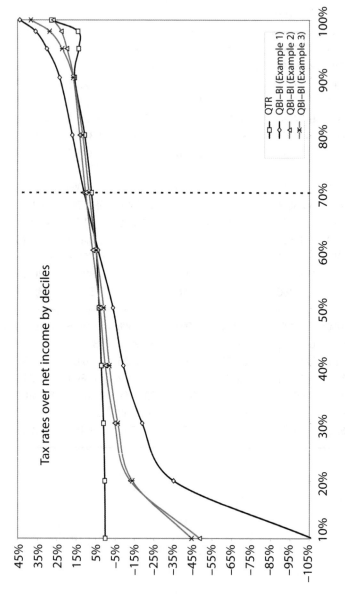

Figure 8.1 Tax rates over net income by deciles

9 BASIC INCOME AND ITS CRITICS

> A basic income has the potential to open up avenues of institutional change necessary for democratisation.
>
> Carole Pateman, 2003

Thus far, I have constructed a number of arguments in favour of Basic Income and have compared it with other measures that have attempted to achieve some of the same results. In passing I have noted several objections. Now, to conclude, I shall look in further detail at eleven of the main criticisms that have been levelled against Basic Income over the last 20 or 25 years. This will also enable me to make a brief summary of all the normative and technical arguments in its favour and to expand on some aspects that I have only briefly mentioned in the earlier chapters. What, then, are these criticisms?

1. Basic Income encourages parasitism.
2. Basic Income will not put an end to the sexual division of labour.
3. Basic Income will mean that some remunerated jobs will be rejected by everyone so that only cheap labour provided by immigrants from poor countries will fill them.

4. Basic Income will exacerbate the dualisation of the working population.
5. Basic Income is an idea that only applies to rich countries or zones, like the European Union or the United States.
6. Basic Income, in being a departure from the idea of income received from performing paid work on the market, discourages people from partaking of the virtues of paid labour. A variation on this theme is that Basic Income undermines the right to (engage in paid) work.
7. Basic Income is inadequate as a measure to put an end to the injustices brought about by the capitalist system.
8. Basic Income involves financing costs that would make it unworkable.
9. Basic Income will constitute a major pull factor for immigration from the poor countries to the rich ones.
10. Basic Income will not fulfil many of its promises if the amount paid out is very small.
11. Basic Income will generate unforeseeable situations.

One interesting way of grouping these eleven criticisms is to put them into categories of those that view Basic Income as (1) ethically undesirable, and (2) technically non-viable, even if perhaps ethically desirable. While it is true that, in some cases, a refined distinction between ethical and technical criticisms is somewhat difficult to achieve (Criticisms 9 and 10, for example, have both ethical aspects and technical components), I still think we can apply this approximate classification. Within the first group we find Criticisms 1–7, and in the second are 8–11 inclusive.

I shall begin with the more numerous set of criticisms, those that view Basic Income as ethically undesirable.

9.1 ETHICAL CRITICISMS

Criticism 1

The first criticism – Basic Income encourages parasitism – is somewhat multifarious, its precise form depending on who is speaking. 'It maintains and encourages layabouts' and 'the workers will be supporting the loafers' are just two examples. Again, this is closely related with the widespread notion that work receiving monetary remuneration is the only kind there is, leading to the related absurdity that not doing remunerated work is the same as not doing anything at all. Hence women (mostly women, of course) who do domestic work are not working and neither are people who are engaged in different kinds of voluntary work. As I explained in some detail in Chapter 4, I believe that the best typology of work is a distinction between three different kinds: remunerated work, domestic work and voluntary work. On the other hand, there are many kinds of 'work' for which remuneration, often very generous, is received yet whose social utility (to use this oft-wielded and rather woolly expression) is non-existent or even negative, as most people would easily agree. Jobs in armies that turn their weapons against their own people, or certain highly paid symbolic positions in both the public and private sectors are examples.

Parasitism is a charge that is not exclusively confined to Basic Income. Any measure that might benefit poorer groups is usually caricatured by the right wing of the political and academic (with a few heroic exceptions) spectrum and management circles as 'encouraging parasitism'. Perhaps the best way to explain what I mean by parasitism is to use the definition of Van Parijs (2003: 207), which also distinguishes it from the phenomenon of the free rider: 'It is bad enough to be a free rider, that is, to benefit from a good while leaving others to bear the full costs of its production. But it is even worse to be a parasite, that is, to benefit from the good while thereby increasing the cost borne by those who produce it.'

The accusation of parasitism is frequently heard when the poor can do something – in very a limited way, of course – that has hitherto been the privilege of the rich. It is generally accepted that rich people can live off inherited wealth without lifting a finger but the idea that the poor should be able to choose, even for a short time, to live without making any contribution is somehow quite shocking for many people. Basic Income, could, for the first time in the history of our species, permit everyone to do what only the richest few have always been able to do: live without making any contribution in return.

The unsatisfied critic may still argue that principle of 'no work, no eat' is a truly just one, as Saint Paul insisted long ago in his Second Letter to the Thessalonians (3: 10–11). In today's world, anyone who does not have land or capital cannot choose to leave a job in the hope of finding something better, unless going hungry or even dying of hunger is some kind of option. Only a miniscule percentage of the population can choose between working for a wage or not. With Basic Income, this possibility would be open to all, at least in a limited way. The reality is that, at present, Paul's 'just' principle, 'If anyone will not work, let him not eat,' applies only to the poor. The rich don't go hungry when they don't work.

I have devoted a good part of Chapter 6 to comparing Basic Income with means-tested subsidies and discussing how they affect the poverty and employment traps in such different ways. Given that it helps to avoid the poverty and unemployment traps, Basic Income would not seem to be very well designed for encouraging parasitism. Furthermore, freeing time from one kind of work – remunerated – can mean that it is easier to invest that time in the other kinds – voluntary and domestic. Believing, despite this, that the time thus freed would be used parasitically by the social majority or a large minority is to have rather peculiar views about human nature. Imagining that a Basic Income would encourage parasitism is to start out from the premise of a human psychology that has no need of stimuli. This simply does not square with what we observe in everyday life. A lot of people who have their economic needs sufficiently covered devote time to training activities, solidarity work and looking after others. It cannot be denied that Basic Income *opens the door to* parasitism, but this is a weaker formulation than the criticism I have been addressing because 'opens the door to' is different from 'encourages'. Yes, it would be a door that is open to anybody and everybody, not just the fortunate few. Unemployment benefits also offer opportunities of parasitism or laziness, and this is why they have perennially been subject to the assault of right-wing detractors who have never been conspicuously bothered by all the opportunities the rich have for being parasites. Basic Income also has its left-wing critics in this regard, but their arguments about parasitism are merely a repetition of the reservations of their right-wing counterparts *vis-à-vis* unemployment benefits: a curiosity, to say no more.

As I noted in Chapter 4 (Section 4.2), other critics say that Basic Income would stimulate an exodus from the job market. Now I shall add a couple of further reflections on this. The extra hours put in voluntarily by many workers, on the one hand, and the remunerated activities in which a lot of retired people are engaged, on the other, are two specific examples that contradict the notion that the availability of labour in the sphere of remunerated work will somehow be jeopardised by the introduction of a Basic Income. First, it is well known that a lot of people put in overtime or extra hours. Neither is it any novelty to point out that a lot of people do overtime, not because their basic needs are not covered, but because they want to enjoy higher levels of consumption or simply to be more comfortably off. In some kinds of work people put in extra hours simply because they want to do the job well. Second, it should be remarked that a lot of workers who have taken early retirement, which is offered by many big companies that want to cut back on staff, continue to engage in remunerated work even though their economic circumstances are quite enviable. When such a lot of workers do overtime and a good many (often prematurely) retired people keep working in the job market, it would seem a bad bet to wager that people wouldn't want to engage in remunerated work if they could count on a Basic Income. Neither should it be forgotten that a Basic Income somewhere near the poverty threshold is quite a lot less than what is received in early retirement payments or by workers who put in extra hours.

To conclude, the fears of the scaremongers about a society of layabouts, dropouts and parasites do not find much support in the evidence we have, nor in what we might reasonably assume.

Criticism 2

The second objection that Basic Income will not put an end to the sexual division of labour is true in a trivial sense. Neither will that division be ended by social housing loans, unemployment benefits, student grants offered by banks, spectator discounts, widows' pensions or annual festivals. Just as no one, as far as I know, has criticised widows' pensions for not resolving the housing problem, nobody should entertain the idea that Basic Income will bring an end to the sexual division of labour. The sexual division of labour is an undesirable social reality whose solution can only come about (assuming we have a clear idea of what 'the' solution is) through a package of measures that is much wider-reaching than Basic Income. It would be a very different thing to say that Basic

Income favours the sexual division of labour, but this criticism has not yet come to my ears.

At this point, I should make a particularly important observation. Basic Income would mean, if it were more or less the amount I suggested in Chapter 8 (at or above the poverty line),[1] the option of not having to work for a wage. This does not contradict what I have said in Chapter 4 and in my response to the first criticism that people will not engage in paid labour. This possibility of not working for a wage might be taken up when people need time to undertake training, or to look after someone or to engage in voluntary work. From the possibility of not working for a wage to the generalisation that nobody would do so, there is a huge conceptual gap, and this is what I have tried to address in my previous response as well as in Chapter 4 (Section 4.2). The option ('right', as Goodhart says – 2006: 25) established by a Basic Income of not having to engage in remunerated work (and this would also be a response to the second criticism) would give women the autonomous material base that would put an end to 'the problematic association between employment, masculinity and citizenship', thereby enabling 'women's equal emancipation' (ibid). I believe that, given this, Basic Income constitutes a very promising doorway to many possibilities which various feminist writers have noted.

Criticism 3

This criticism is closely related to Criticism 9 and they should, perhaps, be considered jointly. According to Criticism 3, a Basic Income would mean that the remunerated jobs that are rejected by everyone who receives a Basic Income could only be filled by cheap labour in the form of immigrants from poor countries. Otherwise, who would do the heaviest and most disagreeable work if a Basic Income were introduced? Since Basic Income is paid to 'each full member or accredited member of a society', this argument simply does not hold water.[2] Whatever one's opinion of the prevailing regulations, immigration from the poor countries is not attracted by jobs in the rich countries that everyone else rejects, but is the result of other factors that have nothing to do with Basic Income. I shall return to this part of the argument when I deal with Criticism 9.

Criticism 4

Basic Income is criticised as being likely to exacerbate the already existing dualisation of the working population. By dualisation I understand the situation in which a society is divided into two large groups of workers. One is made up of those who have secure or stable well-paid work, and the other includes those who frequently move in and out of remunerated work, with badly paid jobs and no guarantee of continuity. (I am speaking here of the situation in rich countries, because a poor country might have a very considerable part of the population living in utter destitution, well outside any parameters of the official economy or the system in general, as 1000 million people do around the world.) Needless to say, the line that divides the two groups is somewhat blurred and there is considerable variation within each group. However, most authors who study the 'dual society' highlight this fragmentation between the sector of the working population that lives on the edge of insecurity with a more or less subsistence wage, and the other part that enjoys secure jobs and high salaries, at least in comparison with the former group.

The statement that Basic Income would exacerbate this duality is somewhat surprising. Dualisation is brought about *inter alia* by a combination of labour legislation, widespread unemployment and new technology (and its management).

Basic Income favours precisely the social group that is worst affected. It would be more reasonable to imagine, as I have been arguing throughout, that the introduction of a Basic Income would favour self-employment, training, salary increases in some disagreeable, heavy or extremely boring kinds of jobs, etcetera. Hence I am not sure where this dualisation argument is coming from. It makes more sense to suppose, on the basis of the arguments I have outlined in Chapter 4, that the work market would be very different from the one we know today in the first decade of the twenty-first century, if a Basic Income were introduced. It would give more muscle to workers in negotiating contracts, increase the salaries of those doing very badly paid work and offer more leeway in freely choosing to do part-time jobs (as opposed to doing them out of necessity). I cannot see how these benefits, amongst others we might add, would favour social dualisation. It would be nearer to the truth to suggest the contrary, that Basic Income would diminish the dualisation of the working population.

Criticism 5

Among the normative objections, Criticism 5, which claims that Basic Income is an idea that only applies to rich countries or zones like the European Union or the United States, is, in a word, wrong. Although the technologically more sophisticated forms of development are certainly to be found in the richer countries, there are also Basic Income sympathisers and proposals for introducing it in countries that are far from highly developed. There is definite and growing interest in Basic Income in countries like Argentina, Brazil, South Africa, Mexico and Colombia, to cite only five that do not belong to the privileged club of the rich countries. What the Argentine writer Lo Vuolo said about the relevance of Basic

Income for all the countries of Latin America, one of the large geographic areas in which people and groups in favour of the proposal are emerging, still holds today:

> Our view is that the proposal of a citizens' income [as Basic Income is called in Argentina] is applicable elsewhere in Latin America for the following reasons: (1) the distribution of wealth tends to be more regressive than in the rich countries, (2) the state reaction against social citizenship and the dismantling of the traditional welfare state is much more advanced and more widely supported in these countries, (3) the problems of social exclusion and its effects in terms of unemployment and poverty are more evident.
>
> (Lo Vuolo, 1995: 41)

Lo Vuolo's argument about Latin America holds true for many zones of the non-rich world.[3]

Criticism 6

The sixth of the normative objections against Basic Income is that, as money that is given without being tied to performing paid work on the market, it would discourage people from enjoying the virtues of paid labour. Although this objection might form part of a more general view of what is deemed to be the central social role of (remunerated) work, I shall try to adhere strictly to the specific criticism.

A diverse range of groups and individuals, of very different inclinations and opinions – Christians, conservatives, paleo-Marxists, and so on – agree that wage work has very special virtues, that it is an instrument of social participation and integration, a key fact of life, and so on. Some people who are bent on finding ever-greater virtues in wage labour would even go as far as to agree with the dubiously poetic assertion of G. Aznar (1994: 99) that, 'To work is to make love with the world.' Similar virtues of paid work tend also to be extolled by university teachers. However, wage earners themselves would not generally agree. This is hardly surprising when even a cursory examination of the matter makes it clear that to attribute such wonders to remunerated work is mere romancing. Claus Offe (1997: 67) acutely asks, 'Why should all the useful activities that human beings are capable of doing be threaded through the eye of the needle of the job contract?' The question follows his remark that:

> different evolutionary facts and tendencies coincide in indicating that the domain of work cannot be subjectively contemplated by all waged workers as the key fact of their lives, the dominant factor from which their interests, conflicts and relationships of social communication derive.

(Offe, 1997: 67)

Let us look more systematically now at the arguments raised against Basic Income by those who celebrate the virtues of remunerated work. The most frequent among them are:

1. Integration through paid work must be the keystone of any struggle against poverty.
2. More basic than the right to an income is the right to social utility.
3. The right to live from one's own work must not be waived.
4. Remunerated work is an indivisible part of social recognition.

Let me now take each of these assertions in turn.

1. This argument doesn't wash. We can see this by breaking it down into two other assertions: (a) it is necessary to struggle against poverty, and (b) paid work is the main (or, in the hard-line version, the only) way of achieving (a). Agreeing with (a) does not necessarily mean agreeing with (b). If remunerated work is not available for anyone who wants it then, if we stay with this argument to the letter, the aim of eliminating or greatly reducing poverty (and social exclusion) will never be achieved. From an empirical point of view, a simple question needs to be posed. Is there paid work available for everyone who wants it? The answer is all too evident: no, not by a long shot.

2. Although it is frequently used by critics of Basic Income, it is difficult to see where the second argument is coming from or where it is going. Social utility does not necessarily or principally have to come from remunerated work. Anna might feel much more socially useful working without pay for the feminist movement than working for a salary in a bank. If she takes time from the former activity in order to work in the latter it is because she is obliged to work for a pay packet in order to support herself. Anyone who wishes to give Anna sermons about the social utility of her work in the bank might come off second best and not only because Anna has little patience with mumbo-jumbo job evangelists. In Chapter 4, I discussed the difficulty of establishing some kind of social hierarchy based on useful work (à la utility theories), and how it is a mere pipe dream to try to find some kind of cardinal order. Trying to respond to the question of how many times more useful it is to work in a bank than in the feminist movement is about as helpful as trying to count angels dancing on the head of a pin.

3. The argument that the right to live from one's own work must not be waived looks very like a problem coming from

a wrong-headed formulation. The Basic Income proposal does not ever oppose the idea that people who want to work for a salary should do so (if they can) but upholds the principle that if they cannot, they should be able to live with dignity. As some academics might say, Basic Income does not prioritise people who want to engage in waged work as opposed to other conceptions of the good life. In plain words, Basic Income is not at all incompatible with wage labour.

4. The fourth argument, one of the more frequent raised by people who contrast the virtues of remunerated work with Basic Income, asserting that wage work is an inseparable part of social recognition, may have been more compelling some decades ago than it is at present. Nowadays, remunerated work is increasingly seen as less important in the lives of the majority of people, as two examples from the past decade illustrate. In a survey conducted in 1997 by Leleux (1998: 60–61), 48 per cent of Belgian workers preferred free time to money. More recently, the latest surveys from the International Social Surveys Programme, based on data collected up to and including 2004, show a similar trend.[4]

In short, the criticism that Basic Income, by being independent of wage work, somehow prevents individuals from exercising and enjoying the virtues of such work, may at first sight appear to be worthy of attention, but in reality does not have much substance.

Criticism 7

This brings us to Criticism 7, which holds that Basic Income is inadequate as a measure to put an end to the injustices brought about by the capitalist system. I hardly need to say that I think this criticism is true in a trivial sense and hence not very interesting. It is uncontroversial because it goes without saying that, with a Basic Income or without one, the capitalist system will continue to be the capitalist system. To give only two examples that characterise the economic and social situation of today's world: first, control of the huge transnational companies would still remain in the hands of very few people (and hence the lives of hundreds of millions of people would continue to be arbitrarily affected by their capitalist priorities) and, second, the international economic organisms would still be exclusively run by the rich countries along the lines that we have seen over the last three decades.

Confronting the immense inequalities that mean an absence of freedom for such a large majority of our species requires other measures. This particular criticism has something in common with Criticism 2, in that both disparage Basic Income for not attaining objectives which it is not designed to attain. Criticising Basic Income because it will not put an end to the injustices of the capitalist system is a bit like sneering at a malaria vaccine because it does not put an end to infant mortality. The relevant response here, once the inconsequentiality of the criticism is noted, would be to ask if malaria vaccines should therefore be withdrawn. What is true of Basic Income is that it *can* change situations that constitute a major part of capitalism's characteristic features. It would mean more freedom for a good part of the population, it would at least partially decommodify the workforce, and it would give more bargaining power to workers, among other improvements that I have already discussed at some length in Chapter 3. Anyone who can grasp what these changes would mean for the capitalist system would appreciate their magnitude, but it would be silly, not to say abusive, to expect more of Basic Income than it is capable of doing.

In Chapter 7 I described what I call the 'crude-political' error of the glib assertion that, since Basic Income is not an anticapitalist measure, there is no point in wasting time and effort on it because if we are going to do anything, it's better to go all out for revolution. This claim, by inference, invalidates any kind of measure at all that is not 'intrinsically anti-capitalist' (assuming it is known what that means).

9.2 TECHNICAL CRITICISMS

The criticisms we find in this group tend to have no normative quarrel with the proposal but judge it technically unviable. However, we still need to bear in mind that there is some degree of overlapping between the two kinds of criticism.

Criticism 8

The first criticism in this group is that the financial costs of Basic Income would make it unworkable. This is not the case, as I have shown in Chapter 8, but I think it is worth returning to the criticism because of the confusion it betrays.

Any significant economic measure will favour some and be detrimental to others (apart from some strictly technical measures – such as including a new product in the Consumer Price Index (CPI) – which do exist but are generally of little importance).[5] Like Basic Income, cutting taxes for the rich, increasing military spending and maintaining the castles and customs of the European monarchies are social options. To give another example of this latter kind of social option, European agricultural subsidies disproportionately benefit some of the wealthiest families in Spain (for example, Samuel Flores, one of the kingdom's biggest landowners, the Botín family, the disgraced banker Mario Conde, another convict banker Emilio Ybarra, oil magnate (*inter alia*) Alfonso Cortina, the Marquis de Valdez Ozores and the Duchess of Alba), with the end result that 126 rich families receive the same amount in EU agricultural subsidies as another 480,000 people.

Depending on how the financing of a Basic Income is carried out, the redistribution of income could benefit (a) people with higher incomes (by dismantling public education and health systems, for example) or (b) people with lower incomes.[6] I believe that I have made it quite clear in the preceding pages that I think that only the second option is of any political (and philosophical) interest.

Asserting that financing a Basic Income is not impossible and that it would not involve exceptional costs is not the same as saying that it is politically uncontroversial. It is difficult to imagine an Emilio Botín, a Rupert Murdoch, a Paris Hilton or a Donald Trump enthusing about Basic Income. When some social sectors gain and others lose, conflict is inescapable. There is nothing special about Basic Income in this regard. Other measures that have been applied over the last two centuries have met greater or lesser resistance and Basic Income is contentious in the same way.

There is no doubt that Basic Income involves financing costs and, when it is at or above the poverty threshold, these costs are not inconsiderable. Yet, with what are we to compare these costs if we are to have an appropriate reference? With the costs of the 'current system' (Goodhart, 2006: 31)? If we make this comparison, Basic Income comes out of it very well unless one is a hard-line admirer of the 'current system'.

Criticism 9

According to Criticism 9, Basic Income would constitute a major pull factor for immigration from the poor countries to the rich ones. The logic here is lugubrious. This claim implies that Basic Income or any measure that brings about an improvement in the condition of the poorest people in the rich countries only increases the gap between them and the poorest people in the poor countries. Social reforms that are worth putting into practice in the rich countries might have arguments for and against them in their own terms, but the argument that they shouldn't be implemented 'because the inhabitants of the poor countries don't have them' is simply untenable. One example that is all too familiar is that the living conditions of women in Afghanistan (under the Taliban regime and the present one) leave nothing to envy. But would it be reasonable to oppose measures that were favourable to women in the European Union, the United States or Australia with the argument that the Afghan women are in a terrible situation and the new measures would only make the gap wider?

Wanting and struggling for public actions and reforms that are thought to improve the lot of inhabitants of the rich countries – and Basic Income will favour not only the poorest members among their citizens – does not necessarily make things worse for the inhabitants of the poor countries. When it comes to other social reforms that are called for in the rich countries (reducing the hours of the working day, salary increases, wider cover with unemployment benefits, early retirement and so on) this argument about increasing the gap between people in rich and poor countries does not usually arise because it is irrelevant. If the tragic conditions that push poor people in the poorest countries to leave their homes and risk their lives travelling in horrendous conditions to seek work elsewhere without any guarantees of finding it were treated as serious concerns, such discussion of the side-effects of Basic Income in rich countries would merely be a red herring.

The pressures to emigrate from the poor to the rich countries arise from the conviction of the least privileged members of the former that it is impossible for them to live in their own country in anything but extreme penury. This being the case, the supposed influence on the 'pull effect' of introducing a Basic Income would be extremely limited. The 'pull effect' – in reality a 'push effect' – will continue to exist as long as people have no real opportunities to live in anything but abject poverty in the poor countries.[7] In this sense it would be more accurate to speak of emigrants than of immigrants.

There are other factors that need to be understood as well. In the early 1990s, the almost total lack of any institutional mechanisms for the social protection of workers in some countries of Southeast Asia and North Africa permitted wage costs that were much lower than those prevailing in the European Union. This gave those countries a significant edge in their competition with the relatively expensive-to-produce European products. Two kinds of argument were raised in response to this situation. The first urged the need to de-structure – 'modernise' it was said – the systems of social protection that had long ago been achieved in the European Union countries so as to recover some of the commercial lead they had lost to the 'newly industrialised countries'. The second stressed the need to respect the significance of these achievements in the social domain, which, in terms of elementary principles of justice, were not to be waived. It was therefore deemed necessary, first, to shift the focus of international commercial competition to other criteria – product quality, for example – and, second, to exhort the working populations of the newly industrialised countries to struggle for the social rights that European workers enjoyed. Although today's circumstances are different, any analysis of the impact of Basic Income on migratory movements must take such issues into account.

At the beginning of 2007, the world's population is almost 7000 million people, and the UN calculates that by the mid twenty-first century it will be in the vicinity of 9100 million.[8]

In the next 45 years, the European Union will see a reduction in its working-age population (15–64 years of age) of almost 50 million people while the population aged 65 and over will increase by 58 million. These variations are highly significant, given that the nominal dependency ratio is expected to be 51 per cent (presently, at 24.5 per cent, it is not even half this);[9] in other words, for each retired person there will only be two people of working age, while the present proportion is four. With regard to immigration, and confining ourselves to cold, hard figures, 'in order to maintain the real dependency ratio constant, 183 million more immigrants will be needed or, in other words, 40 per cent of the population of the European Union in 2050, which will be 454 million.'[10]

The lingering idea that immigrants are a burden to the economy rather than benefiting it is incongruous in the light of recent studies. Guillermo Oglietti (2006) is very clear on this: 'The usual perception that immigration is parasitic needs to be drastically put to rights because the fact of the matter is that the people who receive more than they give are *not* the immigrants'.[11] For the EU15 as a whole, the per capita GDP without immigrants would have been very much less than what was recorded for the period 1994–2004.[12] More specifically, growth would have been 0.23 per cent lower per annum, and even less in some states (1.52 per cent less in Germany and 1.17 per cent less in Italy, for example). In Spain, some 50 per cent of the households established between 2000 and 2005 have a foreigner as the main income earner.

The most succinct way to answer this criticism of the supposed pull effect of Basic Income is to say that people from poor countries are not rushing to reap the benefits of some kind of Basic Income lifestyle but fleeing from life-endangering poverty. Given this reality, the influence that Basic Income might have as a pull effect is utterly irrelevant.[13] Indeed, focusing on supposed pull effects looks like yet another way of dodging any serious consideration of the awful conditions in which the world's poorest people live.

Criticism 10

According to the tenth criticism of Basic Income, it will not fulfil many of its promises if the amount paid out is very small, which is to say a 'partial basic income' (another way of denominating some kind of 'small-quantity' basic income) will not achieve the results of a true Basic Income. I can have no quarrel with this. With a very low 'Basic Income', for instance 50 per cent of the poverty threshold for any particular area, many of the benefits I have been describing in the previous pages either would not be attainable or would only be attained at a much lower level than I have described. As I have argued in Chapter 7 (Section 7.3), the bargaining power of workers *vis-à-vis* the capitalists, or having more time for voluntary work, or greater economic independence for many women who have almost none at present are some of the benefits that a Basic Income could help to achieve. However, if the amount were very small, it is axiomatic that the benefits would be smaller too. There is one argument that some people offer in favour of a 'basic income' of a small amount and this is that its introduction would be the first step along the way towards a Basic Income that is worthy of the name (which requires it to be at or above the poverty threshold). If we accept this view, the core of the argument of Criticism 10 holds intact as long as the transition towards a real Basic Income lasts.[14]

Criticism 11

The last of the objections to Basic Income holds that it can generate unforeseeable situations. In the most vacuous sense, this is certainly true. Any social reform of any importance – and

Basic Income is one – can have unpredictable consequences. Nonetheless, this critical appraisal of Basic Income almost certainly aspires to a less trivial sense in trying to sneak in the idea that the measure would bring about *undesirable* unforeseen situations, which is a rather more contumelious standpoint. It is also illogical. If the situation is unpredictable, we cannot know now whether it will be good or bad because, if we knew, it wouldn't be unpredictable. Yet there might be a prescriptive sense lurking here as well, the idea being that, since we do not know the situations that the introduction of a Basic Income might give rise to, it should not be attempted. I consider this conclusion inadmissible. Of course there will be tensions between the need to act to put an end to specific problems and the unforeseen consequences of this. Not acting is also a decision with unforeseeable consequences.

There may be tension between the unknown results of an action and the need to act in order to remedy particular situations, but one must make political choices on the basis of available information. There is one certain outcome of introducing a Basic Income: the situation of the poorest and most downtrodden among us will improve. In the absence of further information this is more than sufficient reason to act.

* * *

Inequality has never before been as extreme as it is today. In 1900 the average income in the rich countries was four times greater than in the poor countries. Now, in the more or less felicitously named era of globalisation, it is 30 times greater. A recent report by the World Institute for Development Economics of the United Nations University (UNU-WIDER) provides still more shocking data.[15] The world's richest 2 per cent of adults own more than half of global household wealth. The poorest half of its population owns barely 1 per cent of its wealth. Within both rich and poor countries, the gulf between rich and poor is fast growing.

The poor, as I have said, suffer material privation and all the hardships of not being able to consume necessary goods. They are also excluded from the community at large, which means that they are much more vulnerable to different kinds of social pathology. These are the more obvious scourges, but they are also forced to depend on the greed of others, paying thus the terrible price of loss of freedom, and therefore of their very humanity.

Basic Income is a social proposal that can effectively confront a good number of the evils that derive from great inequality and poverty. Not all of them, of course. Yet it *can* guarantee the material conditions of freedom and this is well worth attempting. If *Basic Income: The Material Conditions of Freedom* has demonstrated that this goal is realistically attainable, it will have served its purpose.

NOTES

1. A PROVOCATIVE BUT POSSIBLE PROPOSAL

1. Let us not forget that 'Spain' is a monarchy. The official name of the country is Reino de España (Kingdom of Spain). Since I cannot keep referring to Spain as 'a set of nations including Catalonia and the Basque country', for example, and I do not like using the term Estado Español (Spanish State) I shall use the official denomination here to make my point but henceforth, out of respect for the common usage in English, 'Spain' will suffice.
2. Seewww.etes.ucl.ac.be/BIEN/BI/Definition_temp.htm (last accessed 12 January 2007).
3. Evidently this does not mean that both rich and poor end up gaining with a Basic Income. In most financing proposals, as we shall see in more detail in Chapter 8, the rich lose and the poor gain. Basic Income would be pointless (indeed disastrous, not to say obscene, in my view) if it worked the other way.
4. Alaska Permanent Fund Corporation, 1988.
5. Vanderborght and Van Parijs, 2005, Chapter 1, offer a good summary of this.
6. Seewww.thomaspaine.org/Archives/agjst.html (last accessed 12 January 2007).
7. Russell, 1918. Seewww.globusz.com/ebooks/PropRoad/00000015. htm, Chapter 4 (last accessed 12 January 2007).
8. For a detailed account of this American proposal and its results, see Widerquist, 2004.
9. For an overview of this, see Vanderborght and Van Parijs, 2005, 21 ff.
10. Alperovitz, Gar, 'Another World is Possible', *Mother Jones*, January-February 2005. Seewww.bsos.umd.edu/gvpt/alperovitz/AnotherWorld IsPossible.pdf (last accessed 26 January 2007).

2. NORMATIVE LIBERAL JUSTIFICATIONS

1. Mosterín adds, 'There are different kinds of religious morality but religious ethics (this would be an oxymoron) does not exist. Some so-called ethics committees are simply the vocal organs of a specific kind of religious morality and should be named accordingly, Catholic morality committees, for example. It would then be easier to understand their fussing over issues that are so unworthy of moral consideration as stem cells and the blastulae from which they proceed.'

2. See Amartya Sen, 1992, *Inequality Reexamined*, Oxford, Oxford University Press, p. ix.

3. There is such a huge quantity of literature on the matter, in the form of books, doctoral theses, articles, university class papers and so on, that it would be impossible to elaborate on this in any reasonable amount of space. In any case, it would be futile in terms of the aims of this book. In this chapter, I wish to discuss these theories as simply and clearly as possible with regard to Basic Income and have no desire to muddle the issues by introducing a host of critiques, nuances or comments. However, I shall briefly note some significant aspects of these theories that might serve as some kind of complement for readers who might have a special interest in these points.

4. This stipulation is very debatable but, for our purposes, it is sufficient to note that it asserts that an 'original appropriation' effected by one person is just so long as it is not detrimental to the situation of another person.

5. The very revolutionary Leon Trotsky (1879–1940) who, by any criteria, has little to do philosophically, politically and practically with John Rawls, wrote that in times of scarcity there are queues and when there are queues it is necessary to have police to keep them in order. The history of the USSR turned out to be an unfortunate confirmation of this prediction that was so acute in its early foreboding.

6. In Mosterín's view (2006: 374), 'Rawls proposes consideration of what rational ... but timorous individuals would agree to as a criterion for justifying political norms.'

7. A lexicographic order might be formally defined as follows: $(a1, b1) > (a2, b2)$ if and only if (i) $a1 > a2$ or (ii) if $a1 = a2$, then $b1 > b2$. One obvious example of a lexicographic order is that in which words are presented in a dictionary where the criterion for priority is the series of letters of the alphabet.

8. In a world consisting of four people where the possible distributive schemata were (A) 10:7:4:2; (B) 36:7:6:3; and (C) 80:65:5:4, the maximin criterion would oblige us to choose (C) because the worst-off

person is better-off here than in the other two schemata. This is despite the fact that (A) evidently involves a much more egalitarian distribution than (B) and (C), the latter being the least egalitarian scheme where the richest members are 20 times richer as opposed to (B) and (A), where they are twelve and five times richer respectively.

9.   This is not the place to discuss whether this famous distinction deserves its fame or, in other words, whether it is very interesting or not. For a direct criticism of the distinction between positive freedom and negative freedom, see Bertomeu and Domènech, 2006.

10. The difference in accent between this definition and the one I have proposed in Chapter 1 lies in Van Parijs' unqualified 'work' and my 'paid employment'. The importance of adding 'paid' will become clear in Chapter 4, 'Remunerated Work, Domestic Work and Voluntary Work'.

11. Domènech, 2004, has produced a masterly analysis of this.

12. See Bertomeu and Domènech, 2006.

3.   THE NORMATIVE REPUBLICAN JUSTIFICATION

1.   See Rosenberg, 1921.

2.   See Domènech, 2004: 51.

3.   In 1852 Marx (1818–1883) recognised the long history of the idea when he wrote to Joseph Weydemeyer (1818–1866) that 'no credit is due to me for discovering the existence of classes in modern society or the struggle between them' (Karl Marx and Friedrich Engels, *Selected Correspondence*, Moscow: Progress Publishers, 1965, p. 69).

4.   This quote and those that follow are in the translation of Benjamin Jowett, seeclassics.mit.edu/Aristotle/politics.3.three.html (last accessed 26 January 2007).

5.   Also impressive is the similarity of approach (republican, undoubtedly) on this point between Aristotle and Cicero, on the one hand, and John Locke on the other: 'a free man makes himself a servant to another by selling him for a certain time the service he undertakes to do in exchange for wages he is to receive' (Second Treatise on Government, VII, 85, 1690).

6.   These quotes and those that follow are in the translation of Walter Miller, seewww.stoics.com/cicero_book.html (last accessed 26 January 2007).

7.   For a rigorously documented evaluation of Robespierre, the entire

oeuvre of the historian Albert Mathiez is highly recommended. See in particular Mathiez, 1927 and 1988.

8. A good compendium of his speeches has been produced (in French) by Bosc, Gauthier and Wahnich, 2005. See also http://membres.lycos.fr/discours/discours.htm (last accessed 14 January, 2007).

9. It is true that I could also cite, on their own merits, Jean-Paul Marat (1743–1793) and the young prodigy Louis de Saint-Juste (1767–1794) but citing Robespierre is sufficient for what I wish to discuss.

10. One frequently reads that Immanuel Kant, John Locke and Adam Smith were 'liberals', which is not the case, given the times in which they lived. For detailed accounts of John Locke's conception of republican freedom, see Mundó, 2005 and 2006. For Immanuel Kant, see Bertomeu, 2005b. For Adam Smith, see the excellent doctoral thesis by Casassas, 2005.

11. Both quotes may be found in Lefebvre, 1957: 199–200) See also Domènech, 2004: 92.

12. See Bertomeu and Domènech, 2005.

13. See Immanuel Kant, 2002 [1797].

14. On this point, see Bertomeu, 2005a.

15. See Parker, 1993; Robeyns, 2001; Añón and Miravet, 2004; Pateman, 2003, 2006; XRB-RRB, 2006; Bambrick, 2006.

16. See White, 2003a, 2003b.

17. At the end of his short life, Robespierre seems to have understood 'the inexorable logic by which *fraternité* – as a democratic programme of full and universal *civilisation* of social, economic, family and political life – had to include the full emancipation of women' (Domènech, 2004: 91).

18. See, *inter alia*, Pateman, 2006; Van Parijs, 2006; Domènech and Raventós, 2004.

19. Wright, 2006; Casassas and Loewe, 2001; Raventós and Casassas, 2003; Raventós, 2002; XRB-RRB, 2006.

4. REMUNERATED WORK, DOMESTIC WORK AND VOLUNTARY WORK

1. This definition, though freely modified, is not unlike that offered by Recio, 1988: 22.

2. Public good should not be confused with social good. One social good is the end of all arbitrary interference for each and every member of a

vulnerable social group (see Chapter 3). The *individual good* of being, as a *contingent* and *de facto* matter, protected from arbitrary interference is different from the *social good*, which would mean the end of any *potential* threat to *all* members of a vulnerable group. See Domènech, 2000.

3. Alan Sheahen (2003: 8) expresses this in a very similar way, '[W]hat is work? Just a job? Or anything that's productive? Is a volunteer at a hospital less productive than the same person on an assembly line? Is a mother caring for her children at home less productive than if she were flipping burgers at McDonald's?'

4. Àlex Boso, 2006 uses a similar classification although he includes slave labour.

5. This mention, even in passing, of the neoclassical model, may seem surprising. This is not the time to go into the utilisation of instruments (or 'perversity of instruments', as the case might be). A few words will suffice. I believe that conventional scientific norms and methods should be accepted. Contrasting 'bourgeois science' and 'proletarian science' (supposedly a science that serves bourgeois interests as opposed to an alternative science that instrumentally serves proletarian interests) was a Stalinist invention (used *inter alia* to legitimate more than a few cases of murder, imprisonment and torture and to suffocate for decades in the recently dismantled Soviet Union branches of knowledge as decisive as genetics and mathematical logic). Making a contrast between established – or 'positivist' or 'official' – social theory and 'critical social theory' is not very helpful either. I believe one should reject the idea that 'bourgeois social science' is undialectical, idealist and individualist and that there exists another kind ('critical' or anything else, that is the opposite). In brief, the concerns of any investigation can be formulated in forms that are consistent with normal scientific practice. Any contrast between 'bourgeois science' and 'proletarian science' or 'positive science' and 'critical science' or 'male science' and 'female science' should be rejected, along with the stance that particular methods or analytical instruments are committed to the defence of different kinds of oppression or the 'system'. One of the passages I most admire in Marx is the one where he calls people who mix external considerations with scientific work 'base': 'But when a man seeks to *accommodate* science to a viewpoint which is derived not from science itself (however erroneous it may be) but from *outside, from alien, external interests*, then I call him "base"' (*Capital*, Volume 4 'Theories of Surplus Value', Chapter 9,

emphasis in original). Confusing the social use of scientific knowledge with science is, once again, the source of serious errors.

6. Widerquist, 2004, has produced a detailed summary and evaluation of the NIT experiments in the United States and Canada.

7. A study of this kind, however sophisticated and intellectually honourable it may be, sheds little light on the multiple ramifications that might be entailed with the introduction of a Basic Income for the population as a whole in a large geographic entity such as a state or group of states. As Jon Elster (1987) noted some 20 years ago, and specifically in his arguments against Basic Income, one can perhaps calculate the consequences of the general application of a small reform or the partial application of a large-scale reform but, in general, there are no reasons for believing that in the case of large-scale general application, the results would be the same or similar.

8. Comisiones Obreras (CCOO), 1996.

9. See Noguera, 2001.

10. We shall look at this in detail in Chapter 6.

11. Noguera, 2001.

12. I shall return to this in Chapter 7.

13. See INE (National Statistics Institute) 2004.

14. See Carrasco, 1991, 1992.

15. See Pautassi, 1995: 267.

16. Laura Bambrick, 2006, has recently produced a synthesis as to how Basic Income might affect women in the following six aspects: fostering autonomy, social equality, social integration, social stability, economic efficiency and poverty prevention. These six areas are what Robert Goodin, 1988, notes as the most commonly cited functions of the welfare state.

17. The classification of work into the categories of remunerated, domestic and voluntary work adequately meets the formal criteria of good taxonomy. If we let X be remunerated work, Y be domestic work and Z be voluntary work: (1) No subset of the division can remain empty: $Xi \neq \phi$; $Yi \neq \phi$; $Zi \neq \phi$; (2) The division must be exhaustive so that no element of X, Y or Z can remain outside the division; (3) The division must be exclusive, so that the members of X, Y and Z cannot be members of any other subset. For further details, see Domènech, 2001.

18. It is like political participation, if we understand by this something more than going to vote every few years. Political participation that is not its

own reward does not make sense. Of course, I am not referring to the political bureaucrats who live off politicking. Though I have no doubt that some of them might have an autotelic component in their work, for most bureaucrats, political activity is as instrumental as any other paid work and, moreover, there are usually perks like influence, privileges, plenty of chances to name-drop and show off, etc.

19. Of course we can imagine odd and even outlandish exceptions. For example, A wants to be in closer contact with B (because he is madly in love or thinks that B can help him find a (paid) job he wants, etc.), who spends as much time as possible working for a voluntary association so A joins, believing that it will give him better access to B and that he will look better in B's eyes. Technically speaking, A will be engaging in voluntary work in B's association, but this work will not be autotelic but instrumental because he is doing it for some outside end, unless he is eventually seduced by the work itself and becomes devoted to the cause for its own sake. Again, some volunteers engage in the work, for chances to travel (in the case of third-world solidarity), to overcome personal complexes, or a sexual predator might see it as a way of getting access to defenceless children in an orphanage, for example. We can imagine all kinds of bizarre or pathetic exceptions but, in general, voluntary work is autotelic.

20. Kenneth E. Boulding (1910–1993) adds a third motivation for alternative use of time, noting that the total satisfaction offered by voluntary work would be what an extra hour of work would give, at least to the volunteer, in terms of additional satisfaction either in the activity itself or contemplation of the benefits for others, over what it would require in terms of its being disagreeable and contemplation of alternative uses of the time (Boulding, 1973).

5. POVERTY

1. Although microcredits are now quite fashionable, especially since the 2006 Nobel Peace Prize was awarded to the Bangladeshi founder of the Grameen Bank, Muhammad Yunus, I do not have much faith in this measure as a way of putting an end to poverty. However much the ubiquitous Paul Wolfowitz, now president of the World Bank, enthuses about microcredits, I am more inclined to the view of Walden Bello, who says:

In other words, microcredit is a great tool as a survival strategy, but it is not the key to development, which involves not only massive capital-intensive, state-directed investments to build industries but also an assault on the structures of inequality such as concentrated land ownership that systematically deprive the poor of resources to escape poverty. Microcredit schemes end up coexisting with these entrenched structures, serving as a safety net for people excluded and marginalized by them, but not transforming them. No, Paul Wolfowitz, microcredit is not the key to ending poverty among the 75 million people in Andhra Pradesh.

   Seewww.focusweb.org/microcredit-macro-problems-7.html (last accessed 19 January, 2007).

2. Not to mention how different life would have been for the Indians if the Europeans had not come along.

3. Here, 'social-democratic' refers to the parties that are still members of the so-called Socialist International. These parties have little in common with those that described themselves thus before the First World War and even with those that existed shortly before the Second World War.

4. See Standing,1992, Strengmann-Kuhn, W., 2002, Latta and Peña, 2004, Medialdea and Álvarez, 2005 and Riera, 2006.

5. $8,825 would be equivalent to approximately €6,800 euros (£4,580) and $18,810 to about €14,500 euros (£9,766) respectively in the exchange rates at the beginning of 2007.

6. Also frequently used is the deviation rate I, which represents the distance of the average income of poor individuals from the poverty line. The analytical expression of this index is $I = 1-(\mu_p/z)$ where μ_p is the average income of families below this threshold and z is the value of the threshold. The greater I is, the greater the degree of poverty.

6. THE WELFARE STATE AND BASIC INCOME

1. See, for example, Titmuss, 1958; Abendroth et al, 1986, and Flora, 1986.

2. Here, I am closely following the analysis in Domènech, 2006b.

3. Standing (1999 and 2002) has analysed in great detail the union negotiations that, from within the welfare state, attempted to guarantee the security of workers in seven different areas: the job market (guaranteed

with full employment); employment (high dismissal costs); within the trade (clear possibilities of career improvement within the company); working conditions (accidents at work, regulated hours and so on); qualifications (continuous professional training); income (minimum wage and Social Security) and representation (collective negotiation, right to strike, etc.).

In the United States, this model had its ultimate expression in the highly paternalistic Fordist (after Henry Ford) 'production paradigm'.

4. 'Now, though this state of affairs would be quite compatible with some measure of individualism, yet it would mean the euthanasia of the rentier, and, consequently, the euthanasia of the cumulative oppressive power of the capitalist to exploit the scarcity-value of capital. Interest today rewards no genuine sacrifice, any more than does the rent of land. The owner of capital can obtain interest because capital is scarce, just as the owner of land can obtain rent because land is scarce' (Keynes, 1973).

5. In Domènech's words, 'One illustrative comparison will suffice here. If the Ford executive Robert MacNamara was the strongman of the Kennedy Administration, the Halliburton executive Dick Cheney is George W. Bush's strongman, as was the banker Robert Rubin in the Clinton Administration. The man in charge of the drafting of the European "Constitution" that succumbed to the massive "No" of the French people, the aristocrat Valery Giscard d'Estaing, is none other than the last in the line of the old imperialist financier dynasty that founded the Bank of Indochina. It may seem bizarre but it is not unreasonable that the *New York Times* should now be editorialising about the "class struggle from above".' (Domènech, 2006b: 31)

6. Barr, 1992, can be most highly recommended on market deficiencies.

7. This is not the place to discuss the poverty of the assumptions of this theory of rationality in view of the advances made over the last decades in different scientific disciplines, especially evolutionary biology, cognitive psychology and anthropology. But it is perhaps the place to mention that one of these assumptions is that people process information in a domain-general rather than in a domain-specific form. On the basis of today's knowledge, this is simply false. For a discussion of the way results from the cognitive sciences have cast doubt on folk psychology assumptions, see Barkow et al., 1992, and Hirschfeld and Gelman, 1994. For an introduction to this issue, see Mundó and Raventós, 2000.

8. Pareto's famous Optimum does not fulfil an important desideratum in normative theories: informativity. The more possible social worlds a

normative social theory excludes as undesirable, the more informative it will be. To give a quick idea of this, let us imagine a society consisting of only two people, X and Y. A social product of $1 billion has to be distributed between them. The Pareto efficiency frontier in this society allows all possible distributions of $1 billion between X and Y. If X receives $500,000 and Y does too, this is a Pareto Optimum. But this will also be the case if X receives $1,000 and Y receives $999,999,999,000 or if X receives $2,000 and Y receives $999,999,998,000 , and so on.

9. In the Council of Europe meeting of 20 and 21 March 2003, the Presidency's conclusions alerted against these traps although this was rhetorical and it all remained up in the (hot) air.

10. In this section I shall particularly draw on the work of Arcarons et al., 2005.

11. The taxation system establishes a direct relationship between social contributions and a previously established destination. A quota must be paid and this permits not only the financing of a specific service but also obtaining the 'subjective' (since the individual's contribution guarantees his or access to non-arbitrary financial assistance because it will be directly related with the quota paid and the period over which it has been paid) right to assistance for the subject. Normally, within the taxation model, two options have to be distinguished, the redistributive model and the capitalisation model. In the former, the contributions of the economically active population help to finance the refunds received by another major group, the economically passive sector with the right to a pension, which has given rise to the use of the expression 'intergeneraional solidarity'. The capitalisation option establishes that the beneficiary will receive on retirement the amount that he or she has accumulated throughout his or her working life. This amount includes the contributions previously made and the agreed amount of interest. This option is preferred by private systems.

7   BASIC INCOME IN COMPARISON WITH OTHER PROPOSALS

1. Marco D'Eramo, *'Moderazione infinita: Tratto da 'il manifesto'*, 20 January 2007. Seewww.feltrinelli.it/FattiLibriInterna?id_fatto=7956 (last accessed 25 January 2007).

2. Some people might argue that one should add economic growth to the list of traditional measures against poverty and unemployment. While it might have made sense to do this ten or fifteen years ago, the overwhelming evidence today that poverty and unemployment persist even though growth rates have been considerable means that there is little point in discussing this here.

3. Useful references here are Recio, 1997; Standing, 1999; Atkinson, 2003.

4. In different episodes of everyday life we can find analogous examples that would support the case of the total-liberalisation enthusiasts. A little caustic soda does not unblock the pipes but large quantities can do the job.

5. A graphic way of saying this would be if the reduction of working hours amounts to five hours a week for all the workers in a particular company and the wage cut agreed to is equivalent to two hours, the financing is shared between workers and the company, but the company would be paying more in terms of wage/hour. If the five-hour reduction meant a wage cut equivalent to three hours, then the workers would be paying a proportionally greater cost.

6. See Montes and Albarracín, 1993.

7. This calculation is in keeping with the official description of the unemployed population. This is the population of 16 years of age or older that is not working, is available to work, and is seeking work. People who can start working within a period of two weeks (after the date of the job interview) are deemed to be available. It is considered that there is an effective search for a job when a person has been taking steps in this direction or has attempted to set up his or her own business in the four previous weeks (prior to the interview). Also among the unemployed are included people who have not yet worked and who are waiting to find a job.

    The unemployed population is affected, as of the first quarter of 2001, by the application of a new definition of unemployment established by the European Union in Commission Regulation (EC) 1897/2000 of 7 September 2000. Hence it is not comparable with that of previous periods.

8. According to this widespread and fallacious idea, therefore, if a million hours per day were freed because of a particular reduction of the working day in a hypothetical country, and the working day is eight hours, 125,000 new jobs would be created.

9. See, in this context, the interesting study by Vanderborght, 2006, on the not exactly positive trade union response to Basic Income.

10. See www.direct.gov.uk/MoneyTaxAndBenefits/BenefitsTaxCredits

AndOtherSupport/TaxCredits/TaxCreditsArticles/fs/en?CONTENT_ID
=10010438&chk=IRZWFs (last accessed 6 January 2007).

11. For different approaches to this see Lerner et al, 1999; Sanzo, 2001; Pinilla and Sanzo, 2004; and Arcarons et al, 2005.

12. See http://bostonreview.net/BR25.5/vanparijs.html (last accessed 6 January, 2007).

13. See Le Grand, 1989; Ackerman and Alstott, 1999; Nissan and Le Grand, 2000; Dowding et al, 2003; Wright, 2004.

14. At the beginning of 2007, US$80,000 is worth approximately €60,000, while £10,000 is equal to about €15,000, so that Ackerman and Alstott are proposing a much larger amount than Nissan and Le Grand. Moreover, Nissan and Le Grand establish more restrictions than Ackerman and Alstott on eligibility for the stakeholder grant.

15. Examples of all these positions may be found in the collections of Dowding et al, 2003, and Wright, 2006.

16. I have put 'closer' in inverted commas in order to appeal to the imagination. We might establish that a measure is closer to Basic Income when it is less conditioned in terms of labour contributions or commitments or in terms of means testing, or both.

17. In this particular debate, and quite incomprehensibly, we also find the ingredient of the supposed optimism or pessimism of the participants. When it comes to reasoning, I don't believe for a moment that this business of being more or less 'optimistic' or 'pessimistic' – which will depend on states of mind that in turn can depend on genetic inheritance or lack of neurotransmitters, drugs one might be taking, the state of one's sexual life in relation to previous ambitions, the physical exercise one takes, how one's favourite football team is playing and many other factors – has any bearing on the matter. Leaving aside the well-known trivial meaning of 'seeing things through rose-coloured glasses', an optimist (or pessimist) may see or evaluate or approach any particular situation in very different ways depending on the mechanisms of analysis employed. Yet this focus or evaluation will have little to do with being an optimist (or pessimist), but rather with the analytical tools that are used. A visceral optimist might think that a particular situation is catastrophic while the most hardened pessimist can see another – maybe even the same – situation in the loveliest of colours. An optimist or a pessimist might also be over-endowed or under-endowed with traits such as feeble-mindedness, decrepitude, analytical torpor, compulsive ingenuity, political stolidity or argumentative sagacity, to name but a few. All this will have more bearing on a good or

bad analysis than the temporary or permanent state of pessimism or optimism. Nonetheless, in many crude, academic or jocular debates, the optimistic or pessimistic state of mind immediately appears and is presented as another argument to be triumphantly presented. Or at least to be taken into account. The words 'optimist' and 'pessimist' and their derivatives are sneaked in with all sorts of irrelevancies. Apart from trivial points, optimism and pessimism have nothing to do with a good or bad analysis. Analysis has its own rules, whether we are oozing endorphins or short of them on such-and-such an occasion. Nonetheless, this should not be any obstacle to trying to do anything that one believes is worthy or just. It is hard to improve on Gramsci's (1891–1937) formulation of all this: 'pessimism of the intellect, optimism of the will'.

18. I have discussed this at greater length in Raventós, 2006b.
19. It may be that some Basic Income supporters who commit what I call the 'naive-technical' error tend to be suffer pangs of vertigo because of the radical nature of the proposal. This is humanly possible. Distressed by this vertigo, these people, who frequently have many good qualities although radical thinking is not one of them, want to engage in the Panglossian exercise of making the Basic Income proposal as 'realistic' as they can so that it can be taken on by the political parties (*all* of them if possible), and they convert this into the improbable art of finding similarities between other proposals and Basic Income proper. Needless to say, they commit the other time-worn error of confusing 'realism' with trying to avoid any kind of conflict.

8.   FINANCING

1. See Francis Bacon, 'Of Seditions and Troubles', *The Essays* www. uoregon.edu/~rbear/bacon.html (last accessed 28 January 2007).
2. For the European Union, see Genet and Van Parijs, 1992, and Van Parijs and Vanderborght, 2001. For NAFTA, see Howard, 2006.
3. See Arcarons et al, 2005. Some of the points I shall make in this chapter are a direct translation (from the Catalan) of Chapter 3 of this report and I have also incorporated a considerable amount of new material that was available to us at the end of 2006. Jordi Arcarons thoroughly reviewed this update of our previous work, suggested changes and prepared some of the graphs, which undoubtedly give more precision to my account. I

am also grateful to the other two authors, Àlex Boso and José Antonio Noguera for their help.

4. IRPF (*Impuesto de la Renta de las Personas Físicas*) is direct taxation on personal income. It is a very common form of taxation, although it has differences in its details in every state of the European Union and other geographic zones. Hence, much of what I discuss in this chapter should be of interest for many other geographic areas with taxation systems that resemble that of our study.

5. See the ample bibliography in Arcarons et al, 2005: 100.

6. In this chapter neither of these two additional possibilities is offered. See Arcarons et al, 2005: 148–150.

7. This is equivalent to some US$7,100 per year ($600 per month) or £3,650 per year (£300 per month), according to the exchange rates of January 2007.

8. It should be recalled once again that when we add the cost of a Basic Income for the population not covered in the sample, and deduct the savings in social spending due to the reform, the difference in this first simulation is a positive balance of €492.7 million. Hence, if we include the non-tax-paying population in the sample, the condition of self-financing is still satisfied because the outlay on their Basic Income is covered by this amount.

9. Most advocates of Basic Income in Argentina are grouped in the Red Argentina de Ingreso Ciudadano, one of the twelve official sections that the Basic Income Earth Network has in four continents (www.redaic.org). The Argentine thinkers who have worked most on Citizen Income (as Basic Income is called) are Rubén Lo Vuolo and Alberto Barbeito.

9. BASIC INCOME AND ITS CRITICS

1. Some authors propose a less specific amount than that of the poverty line, but I believe that the general idea is the same. For example Goodhart (2006: 23) says, 'I understand basic income as a serial payment (a social transfer) set at a level assuring that all members of society can meet their subsistence needs for food, clothing, shelter and other basic necessities.'

2. People who are not residing legally in a country (whatever our views about the justice or lack thereof in the conditions imposed for legal residency) would not be able to receive the Basic Income for the simple reason that they would not appear in the Census.

3. See Casassas, Raventós and Wark (2004) for an account of how a Basic Income might stimulate the economy, especially agricultural production in Timor-Leste, one of the world's poorest countries. It could be in large part (over 60 per cent) financed by what the country spends on rice imports today and the rest by proceeds from exploitation of its oil and natural gas reserves. http://www.onlineopinion.com.au/view.asp?article=2332.

4. See, for example, ISSP: http://zacat.gesis.org/; World Values Survey: www.worldvaluessurvey.org/; and British Social Attitudes Survey: www.data-archive.ac.uk/ (last accessed 2 January 2007).

5. The term 'technical measures' is not always as innocuous as it sounds because, in general, right-wing and moderate-left politicians tend to pass off as purely 'technical' measures that have a not inconsiderable political component.

6. A person 'benefits' from a Basic Income with respect to his or her previous situation, when he or she obtains a net additional sum of money. By the same token, Basic Income works to the 'detriment' of a person who ends up with less money. It is evident that somebody living with other people may be individually penalised by the introduction of a Basic Income but still come out ahead because of the possible gains of the people with whom he or she lives. However, since we are unable to come up with any precise figures for such situations (which would mean knowing who holds the purse strings, whether the way of administering the money is fair or not, and so on), the best way to establish the 'winners' and 'losers' is to stay with individual cases, as I have opted to do in Chapter 8.

7. See the interesting document on immigration and Basic Income by Boso et al, 2006. The ILO estimates that 175 million people live outside their country of origin or citizenship (data from 2000). This figure includes migrant workers, permanent immigrants, refugees and their relatives. It is beyond the scope of this discussion to analyse in detail what I must merely note here: in many poor countries the ecosystems have been devastated and their ancestral economic systems completely disrupted. If the system were not so tragic, any well-informed person would laugh at the idea that emigration from the poor countries is really a 'quest for a better life'. The reality is that the emigrants do not want to die or suffer the effects of severe hunger.

8. See http://esa.un.org/unpp (last accessed 2 January, 2007).

9. The nominal dependency ratio measures the number of retired people compared with those of working age.

10. Dehesa, 2006: 72.

[213]

11. See Guillermo Oglietti, 2006, 'Los beneficios económicos de la inmigración en España', *sinpermiso*, 15 October, www.sinpermiso.info/ articulos/porautor/# (last accessed 23 January 2007).

12. See *Informe Semestral I/2006* (Half-yearly Report I/2006), July 2006, published by la Caixa de Catalunya.

13. Some ironies inherent in this pull-factor perspective are not lost on Mike Davis, 2006, when he writes of the frontier between the United States and Mexico. 'Nativism, today as in the past, is bigotry as surreal caricature, reality stood on its head. The ultimate irony, however, is that there really is something that might be called a "border invasion," but the Minutemen's billboards are on the wrong side of the freeway. What few people, outside of Mexico at least, have bothered to notice is that while all the nannies, cooks, and maids have been heading North to tend the luxury lifestyles of irate Republicans, the Gringo hordes have been rushing South to enjoy glorious budget retirements and affordable second homes under the Mexican sun.' See 'When the Gringos Go Down South', www.socialistreview. org.uk/article.php?articlenumber=9842 (last accessed 24 January 2007).

14. It is worth recalling at this point that in Chapter 7 (Section 7.3.1) I discussed the question of how near we might be to a Basic Income (or how far from it) with regard to more or less similar transitory measures that might be applied.

15. Seewww.wider.unu.edu/ (last accessed 24 January 2007).

BIBLIOGRAPHY

Abendroth, W., Forsthoff, E. and Doehring, K. (1986) *El Estado social* (Barcelona: Grijalbo).

Ackerman, B. (1993) *La justicia social en el Estado liberal* (Madrid: Centro de Estudios Constitucionales).

Ackerman B. and Alstott, A. (1999) *The Stakeholder Society* (New Haven: Yale University Press).

Alaska Permanent Fund Corporation (1988) 'Wealth Management: A Comparison of the Alaska Permanent Fund and Other Oil-Generated Savings Accounts around the World', *The Trustee Papers*, No. 5, April.

Alba, A. (2000) *La riqueza de las familias: Mujer y mercado de trabajo en la España democrática* (Barcelona: Ariel).

Albarracín, J. and Montes, P. (1993) 'El debate sobre el reparto del empleo', *Viento Sur*, No. 12.

Añón, M.J. and Miravet, P. (2004) 'El derecho a un ingreso y la cuestión social de las mujeres europeas', in J. Martínez Ridaura and Mariano J. Aznar (eds), *Discriminación y diferencia* (Valencia: Tirant lo Blanc).

Arcarons, J, Boso, À, Noguera, J.A. and Raventós, D. (2005) *Viabilitat i impacte d'una Renda Bàsica de Ciutadania per a Catalunya* (Barcelona: Mediterrània-Fundació Jaume Bofill).

Aristotle (1997) [350 BC] *Politics*, http://classics.mit.edu/Aristotle/politics.html (translation by Benjamin Jowett).

Atkinson, A.B. (1993) 'Participation Income', *Citizen's Income Bulletin*, No. 16.

Atkinson, A.B. (1996) 'The Case for a Participation Income', *The Political Quarterly*, Vol. 67.

Atkinson, A.B. (2003) 'Labour Market Flexibility and the Welfare State', in R. Arnott, B. Greenwald, R. Kanbur and B. Nalebuff, (eds), *Economics for an Imperfect World* (Cambridge Mass.: MIT Press).

Ayala, L.(1998) 'Cambio demográfico y pobreza', in EDIS et al. *Las condiciones de vida de la población pobre en España. Informe general* (Madrid: Fundación Foessa).

[215]

BIBLIOGRAPHY

Aznar, G. (1980) *Tous a mi-temps* (Paris: Seuil).

Aznar, G. (1994) *Trabajar menos para trabajar todos* (Madrid: Ediciones Hoac).

Bambrick, L. (2006) 'Wollstonecraft's Dilemma: Is a Citizen's Income the Answer?', *Citizen's Income Newsletter*, No. 2.

Barkow, J., Cosmides, L. and Tooby, J. (eds) (1992) *The Adapted Mind: Evolutionary Psychology and the Generation of Culture* (Oxford: Oxford University Press).

Barr, N.A. (1992) 'Economic Theory and the Welfare State: A Survey and Interpretation', *Journal of Economic Literature*, No, 30.

Bator, F. (1958) 'The Anatomy of Market Failure', *Quarterly Journal of Economics*, Vol. 72, No. 2.

Bertomeu, M.J. (2005a) 'Republicanismo y propiedad', *El Viejo Topo*, No. 207.

Bertomeu, M.J. (2005b) 'Las raíces republicanas del mundo moderno: en torno a Kant', in M.J. Bertomeu, A. Doménech, A. and A. de Francisco (eds), *Republicanismo y democracia* (Buenos Aires: Miño y Dávila Editores).

Bertomeu, M.J. and Domènech, A. (2005) 'Algunas observaciones sobre método y substancia normativa en el debate republicano', in M.J. Bertomeu, A. Doménech, A. and A. de Francisco (eds), *Republicanismo y democracia* (Buenos Aires: Miño y Dávila Editores).

Bertomeu, M.J. and Domènech, A. (2006) 'El republicanismo y la crisis del rawlsismo metodológico (Nota sobre método y substancia normativa en el debate republicano)', *Isegoría* (forthcoming).

Bertomeu, M.J., Domènech, A. and Raventós, D. (2005) 'La propuesta de la Renta Básica de ciudadanía', *El Dipl*ó (Argentine edition), July.

Bosc, Y., Gauthier, F. and Wahich, S. (eds) (2005) *Por la felicidad y por la libertad (discursos de Robespierre)* (Barcelona: el Viejo Topo).

Boso, A. (2006) 'Formas de trabajo en el capitalismo: Una aproximación conceptual' (Barcelona: Congrés de Joves Sociòlegs).

Boso, A., Larrinaga, I. and Vancea, M. (2006) 'Basic Income for Immigrants Too: a Model of Global Justice for the 21st Century?' (Durban: 16th World Congress of Sociology).

Boulding, K.E. (1973) *The Economy of Love and Fear: A Preface to Grants Economics* (Belmont, Calif.: Wadsworth).

Brugué, Q., Gomà, R. and Subirats, J. (2002) 'De la pobreza a la exclusión social', *Revista Internacional de Sociología*, No. 33.

Carrasco, C. (1991) *El trabajo doméstico, un análisis económico* (Madrid: Ministerio de Trabajo y Seguridad Social), doctoral thesis.

Carrasco, C. (1992) 'El trabajo de las mujeres: producción y reproducción', *Cuadernos de Economía,* Vol. 20, No. 57/58.

BIBLIOGRAPHY

Carrasco, C., Alabart, A., Mayordomo, M. and Montagut, T. (1997) *Mujeres, trabajos y políticas sociales: una aproximación al caso español* (Madrid: Ministerio de Trabajo y Asuntos Sociales. Instituto de la Mujer, No. 51).

Casassas, D. (2005) *Propiedad y comunidad en el republicanismo comercial de Adam Smith: el espacio de la libertad republicana en los albores de la gran transformación* (Barcelona: Universitat de Barcelona).

Casassas, D. and Loewe, G (2001) 'Renta Básica y fuerza negociadora de los trabajadores', in D. Raventós (ed.), *La Renta Básica. Por una ciudadanía más libre, más igualitaria y más fraterna* (Barcelona: Ariel).

Casassas, D. and Raventós, D. (2007) 'Property and Republican Freedom: Basic Income as a Right of Existence in Contemporary Societies', *Basic Income Studies* (forthcoming).

Cicero, Marcus Tullius (1913) [44 BC] *De Officiis* (translated by Walter Miller), Loeb Edition (Cambridge: Harvard University Press), www.stoics, com/cicero_book.html.

Comisiones Obreras (CCOO) (1996) (Various authors) *Jornades sobre repartiment del treball i treball d'igual valor* (Madrid: Secretaría confederal de la mujer de CCOO).

Dehesa, G. (2006) 'La inmigración no ha hecho más que empezar', *El País*, 19 September.

Domènech, A. (1989) *De la ètica a la política (de la razón erótica a la razón inerte)* (Barcelona: Crítica).

Domènech, A. (1991): 'Summum ius summa iniuria', in C. Thiebaut (ed.), *La herencia ética de la Ilustración* (Barcelona: Crítica).

Domènech, A. (2000) 'Solidaridad', *Viento Sur*, No. 50.

Domènech, A. (2001) 'Conceptos Metodológicos Básicos', in J. Mundó (ed.), *Filosofía y epistemología* (Barcelona: Fundació per a la Universitat Oberta de Catalunya).

Domènech, A. (2004) *El eclipse de la fraternidad* (Barcelona: Crítica).

Domènech, A. (2006a) 'Azarosas élites bajo palabra de honor', *Sin Permiso*, No. 1.

Domènech, A. (2006b) 'República y socialismo, también para el siglo XXI', *Sin Permiso*, No. 1.

Domènech, A. and Raventós, D. (2004) 'La Renta Básica de Ciudadanía y las poblaciones trabajadoras del primer mundo', *Le Monde diplomatique* (Spanish edition), No. 105.

Dowding, K., De Wispelaere, J. and White, S. (eds) (2003) *The Ethics of Stakeholding* (London: Palgrave Macmillan).

Eagleton, T. (2003) *After Theory* (New York: Basic Books).

BIBLIOGRAPHY

Elster, J. (1987) 'Comment on Van der Veen and Van Parijs', *Theory and Society*, No. 15.

Ferry, J-M. (1995) *L'Allocation universelle: Pour un revenu de citoyenneté* (Paris: Cerf).

Flora, P. (ed.) (1986) *Growth to Limits: The Western European Welfare Status since World War II* (Berlín: De Gruyter).

France, A. [Thibault, J.A.] (1923) [1894] *Le Lys rouge* (Paris: Calmann-Lévy).

Frank, R.H. (1999) *Luxury Fever: Why Money Fails to Satisfy in an Era of Excess* (New York: Free Press).

Friedman, M. (1962) *Capitalism and Freedom* (Chicago: University of Chicago Press).

Gamel, C., Balsan, D. and Vero, J. (2006) 'The Impact of Basic Income on the Propensity to Work: Theoretical Issues and Microeconometric Results', *Journal of Socio-Economics*, Vol. 35, No. 3.

Gauthier, D. (1994) *La moral por acuerdo* (Barcelona: Gedisa).

Genet, M. and Van Parijs, P. (1992) 'Eurogrant', *Basic Income Research Group Bulletin*, No. 15.

Gershuny, J.I. (2000) *Changing Times: Work and Leisure in Postindustrial Society* (Oxford: Oxford University Press).

Goodhart, M. (2006) '"None So Poor that He is Compelled to Sell Himself": Democracy, Subsistence, and Basic Income', in Lanse Minkler and Shareen Hertel (eds), *Economic Rights* (forthcoming, Cambridge University Press).

Goodin, R.E. (1988) *Reasons For Welfare* (New Jersey: Princeton University Press).

Gorz, A. (1997) 'Salir de la sociedad salarial', in A. Recio, C. Offe and A. Gorz (eds), *El paro y el empleo: enfoques alternativos* (Valencia: Germania).

Heinze, R.G. et al. (1992) 'Diferenciación de intereses y unidad sindical', in C. Offe (ed.), *La sociedad del trabajo. Problemas estructurales y perspectivas de futuro* (Madrid: Alianza).

Hirschfeld, L.A. and Gelman, S.A. (1994) *Mapping the Mind: Domain Specificity in Cognition and Culture* (Cambridge: Cambridge University Press).

Hirschman, A.O. (1991) *Retóricas de la intransigencia* (México: FCE).

Instituto Nacional de Estadística (2004) 'Encuesta de empleo del tiempo 2002–2003', www.ine.es/prensa/np333.pdf.

Kant, I. (2002) [1785] *Groundwork of the Metaphysics of Morals* (translated and edited by Mary J. Gregor) (Cambridge: Cambridge University Press).

Keynes, J.M. (1973) *The General Theory of Employment, Interest and Money* (London: Macmillan, St. Martin's Press for the Royal Economic Society).

[218]

Kymlicka, W. (1995) *Filosofía política contemporánea* (Barcelona: Ariel).

Latta, M. and Peña, R. (2004) *Working Poor in the European Union* (Dublín: European Foundation for the improvement of Living and Working Conditions).

Lefebvre, G. (1957) *Les Thermidoriens: Le Directoire* (Paris: Armand Colin).

Le Grand, J. (1989) 'Markets, Welfare and Equality,' in J. Le Grand and S. Estrin (eds), *Market Socialism* (Oxford: Oxford University Press).

Leleux, C. (1998) *Travail ou revenue?* (Paris: Cerf).

Lerner, S., Clark C. and Needham, W.N. (1999) *Basic Income: Economic Security for All Canadians* (Toronto: Between the Lines).

Lo Vuolo, R. (ed.) (1995) *Contra la exclusión:La propuesta del ingreso ciudadano* (Buenos Aires: Miño y Dávila).

Locke, J. (1960) [1690] *Two Treatises on Government* (ed. P. Laslett) (Cambridge: Cambridge University Press).

Marx, A. and Peeters, H. (2004) 'Win for Life. What, if Anything, Happens after the Introduction of a Basic Income?' (Barcelona: Basic Income European Network, 10th International Congress).

Marx, K. (1981) *Obras escogidas de Marx y Engels* (3 volumes) (Moscow: Progress).

Mathiez, A. (1927) *The Fall of Robespierre and Other Essays* (New York: Alfred A. Knopf).

Mathiez, A. (1988) *Études sur Robespierre* (Paris: Messidor/Editions sociales).

McKinnon, C. (2006) 'A Scandalous Proposal: Ethical Attractions of Basic Income', *Basic Income Studies*, No. 1.

Méda, D. (1998) *El trabajo: Un valor en peligro de extinción* (Barcelona: Gedisa).

Medialdea, B and Álvarez, N. (2005) 'Ajuste neoliberal y pobreza salarial: los 'working poor' en la Unión Europea', *Viento Sur*, No. 82.

Montes, P. and Albarracín J. (1993) 'El debate sobre el reparto del empleo', *Viento Sur*, No. 12.

Mosterín, J. (2006) *La naturaleza humana* (Pozuelo de Alarcón: Gran Austral).

Mundó, J. (2005) 'Autopropiedad, derechos y libertad (¿debería estar permitido que uno pudiera tratarse a sí mismo como a un esclavo?)', in M.J. Bertomeu, A. Domènech and A. de Francisco (eds), *Republicanismo y democracia* (Buenos Aires: Miño y Dávila Editores).

Mundó, J. (2006) 'Locke y Aristóteles', in M.J.Bertomeu, E. Di Castro and A. Velasco (eds), *La vigencia del republicanismo* (México: Universidad Nacional Autónoma de México).

BIBLIOGRAPHY

Mundó, J. and Raventós, D. (2000) 'Fundamentos cognitivo-evolucionarios de las ciencias sociales', *Revista Internacional de Sociología*, No. 25.

Nissan, D. and Le Grand, J. (2000) *A Capital Idea: Start Up Grants for Young People* (London: Fabian Society).

Noguera, J.A. (2001) 'Renta Básica o 'trabajo básico'? Algunos argumentos desde la teoría social', paper given at the *I Simposio de la Renta Básica* (First Basic Income Symposium, Barcelona, 8 June 2001).

Nozick, R. (1974) *Anarchy, State, and Utopia* (Oxford: Basil Blackwell).

Offe, C. (1997) '¿Pleno empleo? Para la crítica de un problema mal planteado', in A. Recio, C. Offe and A. Gorz (eds), *El paro y el empleo: enfoques alternativos* (Valencia: Germania).

Parker, H. (1993) *Citizen's Income and Women*, BIRG Discussion Paper 2. (London: Citizen's Income).

Pateman, C. (2003) 'Freedom and Democratization: Why Basic Income is to be Preferred to Basic Capital', in K. Dowding, J. de Wispelaere and S. White (eds), *The Ethics of Stakeholding* (Basingstoke: Palgrave Macmillan).

Pateman, C. (2006) 'Democratizing Citizenship: Some Advantages of a Basic Income', in B. Ackerman, A. Alstott and P. Van Parijs (eds), *Redesigning Distribution* (London/New York: Verso).

Pautassi, L. (1995) '¿Primero... las damas? La situación de la mujer frente a la propuesta del ingreso ciudadano', in Rubén Lo Vuolo (ed.), *Contra la exclusión: La propuesta del ingreso ciudadano* (Buenos Aires: Miño y Dávila).

Pettit, P. (1997) *Republicanism: A Theory of Freedom and Government* (Oxford: Oxford University Press).

Pinilla, R. and Sanzo, L. (2004) *La Renta Básica: Para una reforma del sistema fiscal y de protección social*, Working Paper 42/2004 (Madrid: Fundación Alternativas).

Ramos, F. (2003) *Autorrealización y trabajo* (Barcelona: Universitat de Barcelona).

Ramos, F. (2004) 'Políticas de empleo', in C. Ruiz Viñals (ed.), *Políticas sociolaborales: un enfoque pluridisciplinar* (Barcelona: UOC).

Raventós, D. (1999) *El derecho a la existencia* (Barcelona: Ariel).

Raventós, D. (2002) 'Detrás de la desigualdad hay un problema de libertad o "los que viven con permiso de otros"', *El valor de la palabra – Hitzaren Bailoa*, No. 2.

Raventós, D. (2006a) 'Prologue', in Y. Vanderborght and P. Van Parijs, *La Renta Básica* (Barcelona: Paidós).

Raventós, D. (2006b) 'Cinco años no es nada: glosas a una vieja y buena reseña', *Viento Sur*, No. 85.

Raventós, D. and Casassas, D. (2003) 'La Renta Básica y el poder de nego-
ciación de "los que viven con permiso de otros"', *Revista internacional
de sociología*, No. 34.

Rawls, J. (1971) *A Theory of Justice* (Cambridge, Mass.: Harvard University
Press).

Rawls, J. (1988) 'The Priority of Right and Ideas of the Good', *Philosophy
and Public Affairs*, Vol. 17, No. 4.

Rawls, J. (1996) *El liberalismo político* (Barcelona: Crítica).

Rawls, J. (2001) *Justice as Fairness: A Restatement* (ed. Erin Kelly)
(Cambridge, Mass.: Harvard University Press).

Recio, A. (1988) *Capitalismo y formas de contratación laboral* (Madrid:
Ministerio de Trabajo y Seguridad Social).

Recio, A. (1997) *Trabajo, personas, mercados* (Barcelona: Icaria-Fuhem).

Reid, M. (1934) *Economics of Household Production* (New York: John Wiley).

Riera, A. (2006) 'Working poors made in Europe', www.legrandsoir.info/
article.php3?id_article=3579.

Robespierre, M. (1958–67) *Oeuvres* (Paris: Société des Études Robespierristes).

Robeyns, I. (2001) 'An Income of One's Own', *Gender and Development*,
Vol. 9, No. 1.

Rosenberg, A. (1921) *Demokratie und Klassenkampf im Altertum* (Leipzig:
Bielefeld)

Russell, B. 1966 [1918] *Roads to Freedom: Socialism, Anarchism and
Syndicalism* (London: Unwin).

Sacristán, M. (1983) 'Karl Marx', in *Sobre Marx y marxismo* (Barcelona: Icaria).

Sanzo, L. (2001) 'Líneas de actuación para el impulso de una Política de
Garantía de Ingresos', paper presented at the *I Simposio de la Renta
Básica* (First Basic Income Symposium, Barcelona, 8 June).

Sen, A. (1976) 'Poverty: An Ordinal Approach to Measurement', *Econometrica*,
Vol. 44, No. 2.

Sen, A. (1980) 'Equality of what?' in S. McMurrin (ed.), *Tanner Lectures on
Human Values* (Cambridge: Cambridge University Press).

Sen, A. (1992) *Inequality Reexamined* (Cambridge, Mass.: Harvard University
Press).

Sheahen, A. (2003) *Does Everyone Have The Right To A Basic Income Guarantee?* (New York: United States Basic Income Guarantee, 2nd Conference).

Standing, G. (1992) 'Meshing Labour Market Flexibility with Security: An
Answer to British Unemployment?', *International Labour Review*, No. 125.

Standing, G. (1999) *Global Labor Flexibility: Seeking Distributive Justice*
(Basingstoke: Macmillan).

BIBLIOGRAPHY

Standing, G. (2002) *Beyond the New Paternalism: Basic Security as Equality* (London: Verso).

Steiner, H. (1992) 'Three Just Taxes', in P. Van Parijs (ed.), *Arguing for Basic Income* (London: Verso).

Ste. Croix, G.E.M. (1981) *The Class Struggle in the Ancient Greek World From the Archaic Age to the Arab Conquests* (London: Duckworth).

Stiglitz, J. (2003) *The Roaring Nineties: A New History of the World's Most Prosperous Decade* (New York: W.W. Norton).

Stiglitz, J. (2006) *Making Globalization Work* (New York: W.W. Norton).

Strengmann-Kuhn, W. (2002) 'Working Poor in Europe: A Partial Basic Income for Workers?' (Geneva: Basic Income European Network, 9th International Congress).

Subirats, J. (ed.) (2004) *Pobreza y exclusión social: Un análisis de la realidad española y europea* (Barcelona: Publicacions de la obra social de La Caixa).

Titmuss, R. (1958) *Essays on the Welfare State* (London: Allen and Unwin).

Tobin, J. (1965) 'On the Economic Status of the Negro', *Daedalus*, Vol. 94, No. 4.

US Bureau of Labor Statistics (2003) 'A Profile of Working Poor, 2003', Report 983. www.bls.gov/cps/cpswp2003.pdf.

Vanderborght, Y. (2006) 'Why Trade Unions Oppose Basic Income', *Basic Income Studies* No. 1.

Vanderborght, Y. and Van Parijs, P. (2005) *L'allocation universelle* (Paris: La Découverte).

Van der Veen, R. (2003), 'Assessing the Unconditional Stake', in K. Dowding, J. De Wispelaere, J. and S. White (eds), *The Ethics of Stakeholding* (London: Palgrave Macmillan).

Van der Veen, R. and Van Parijs, P. (1986) 'A Capitalist Road to Communism', *Theory and Society*, Vol. 15, No. 5.

Van der Veen, R. and Van Parijs, P. (2006) 'A Capitalist Road to Global Justice: Reply to Another Six Critics', *Basic Income Studies*, No. 1.

Van Parijs, P. (1991) *Qu'est-ce qu'une société juste?* (Paris: Le Seuil).

Van Parijs, P. (1995) *Real Freedom for All: What (if Anything) Can Justify Capitalism?* (Oxford: Oxford University Press).

Van Parijs, P. (1996) 'L'allocation universelle contre le chômage', *Revue Française des Affaires Sociales*, Vol. 50, No. 1.

Van Parijs, P. (2000) 'A Basic Income for All', *Boston Review*, Vol. 25, No. 5.

Van Parijs, P. (2003) 'Hybrid Justice, Patriotism and Democracy: A Selective Reply', in A Reeve and A. Williams (eds), *Real Libertarianism Assessed: Political Theory after Van Parijs* (Houndmills: Palgrave Macmillan).

BIBLIOGRAPHY

Van Parijs, P. (2006) 'Basic Income versus Stakeholder Grants: Some Afterthoughts on How Best to Redesign Distribution', in B. Ackerman, A. Alstott and P. Van Parijs (eds), *Redesigning Distribution* (London/New York: Verso).

Van Parijs, P. and Vanderborght, Y. (2001) 'From Euro-Stipendium to Euro-Dividend', *Journal of European Social Policy*, Vol. 11, pp. 342–6.

Vonnegut, K. (1968), 'Harrison Bergeron', in *Welcome to the Monkey House* (New York: Delacorte).

White, S. (2003a) *The Civic Minimum* (Oxford: Clarendon).

White, S. (2003b) 'Fair reciprocity and Basic Income', in A. Reeve and A. Williams (eds), *Real Libertarianism Assessed: Political Theory after Van Parijs* (Houndmills: Palgrave Macmillan).

Widerquist, K. (2004) 'A Failure to Communicate: The Labour Market Findings of the Negative Income Tax Experiments and their Effects on Policy and Public Opinion', in G. Standing (ed.), *Promoting Income Security as a Right: Europe and North America* (London: Anthem Press).

Wright, E.O. (1994) *Interrogating Inequality: Essays on Class Analysis, Socialism and Marxism* (London/New York: Verso).

Wright, E.O. (1997), '*Reflexiones sobre socialismo, capitalismo y marxismo*' (Palma de Mallorca: Contextos (CCOO)).

Wright, E.O. (ed.) (2004) *Basic Income vs. Stakeholder Grants*, monographic number of *Politics and Society*, Vol. 32, No. 1.

Wright, E.O. (2006) 'Basic Income as a Socialist Project', *Basic Income Studies* No. 1.

XRB-RRB (Xarxa Renda Bàsica) (2006) *Preguntes i respostes sobre la renda bàsica* (Barcelona: XRB-RRB).

INDEX

ɛ _

INDEX

INDEX

INDEX